Financial Institution Advantage and the Optimization of Information Processing

WILEY & SAS BUSINESS SERIES

The Wiley & SAS Business Series presents books that help senior-level managers with their critical management decisions.

Titles in the Wiley & SAS Business Series include:

For more information on any of the above titles, please visit www.wiley.com.

Financial Institution Advantage and the Optimization of Information Processing

Sean C. Keenan

WILEY

Library of Congress Cataloging-in-Publication Data:

Keenan, Sean C., 1961-
  Financial institution advantage & the optimization of information processing /
Sean C. Keenan.
     pages cm. – (Wiley & SAS business series)
  Includes bibliographical references and index.
  ISBN 978-1-119-04417-8 (cloth); ISBN 978-1-119-05304-0 (ebk);
ISBN 978-1-119-05322-4 (ebk)
  1. Financial services industry–Data processing. 2. Financial services industry–
Information technology. 3. Financial institutions–Management. I. Title. II. Title:
Financial institution advantage and the optimization of information processing.
  HG173.K397 2015
  332.10285–dc23
                                                                    2014041589

Printed in the United States of America

10 9 8 7 6 5 4 3 2 1

For Sage & Coleman.

Contents

Introduction

At its most basic level, a financial institution is composed of four things: a brand, a collection of personnel, some physical assets, and analytic (information) assets. The last category includes things like data, data processing capabilities, statistical models of various kinds, and other analytic and reporting capabilities. This categorical breakdown is simplistic, and not exactly clean. For example, there is an overlap between physical assets and data processing capabilities: Are the computers themselves physical assets or information assets? Overlap also exists between personnel and analytic methods: Does a buy or sell decision stem from an analytic method or from a person who makes buy and sell decisions? In spite of this lack of clarity, using this categorization—even in its most simplistic form—can help to frame the crucial underlying competitive issues facing financial institutions today. These issues can be summarized as follows:

1. If you have a strong brand, great, try to preserve it. If not, try to build one. But how?
2. If you have great personnel, great, try to retain them. If not, try to attract them. But how?
3. Physical assets are highly fungible, depreciate rapidly, and matter little, except insofar as they contribute to brand strength and the ability to attract and retain talent.
4. Information assets, actively and effectively managed, create competitive advantages and improved financial results. This helps to build brand strength and attract top talent.

Under this simple view, a financial institution that wants to be more competitive and more successful needs to focus assiduously on more effective management of information assets, including data acquisition and information processing. The goal of this book is not to describe the ideal state for any particular aspect of any business process within an actual financial institution. Rather, its goal is to suggest a prioritization of certain capabilities as critical *strategic* core competencies, provide some thoughts about *better* (if not *best*) practices, and to suggest a set of mechanisms for self-evaluation. In other words, how does an institution evaluate its information processing capability and take practical steps toward improving it?

Nearly every month the media report cases of major blunders by financial institutions in trading, reporting of financial information, and mishandling of customer information, along with censures from regulators caused by failures in data management or information processing. While these high-profile events may be signaling something about the capabilities of specific firms or about the average level of capability within the industry as a whole (raising concerns about the potential frequency of future costly gaffes), the underlying issue is not about the cost of isolated blunders. Instead, it is about the efficiency and effectiveness of the tens of thousands of tasks that financial institutions need to perform every day in order to earn their right to exist. The deeper question that ought to be asked by investors, managers, and other market participants is how well can these institutions develop, market, and manage financial products and services relative to their peers, given that these activities are critically dependent on information processing capabilities?

Importantly, financial institutions need not only be concerned about direct competition from more capable peers. They also need to be concerned about encroachment from more capable firms in tangential or even unrelated industries. One obvious threat is from firms whose core competency is squarely in Big Data management and information processing generally. These would include firms like Amazon, Yahoo, and Google, but even firms with other closely related strengths, such as logistics, can be threats to financial institutions that fall behind. For a powerful example, see "Wal-Mart Dives Deeper in Banking," *Wall Street Journal*, April 18, 2014. To cite another example, Facebook now boasts more than 1.3 billion customers (it reported it had 20 million in 2007 and 200 million in 2009), and it is said that the company has more information about its customer base than any firm in history. How difficult would it be for Facebook, assuming it was committed to that strategy, to launch Facebank? And how might that development further change the competitive landscape for financial services? The answer to the former question may already be known. According to *American Banker,* an Accenture-conducted survey in March of 2014 of 3,846 bank customers in North America revealed that:

> Almost half (46 percent) of consumers aged 18 to 34 said that if PayPal offered banking services, they would want to use them. About 40 percent said the same about Google and 37 percent favored Amazon.... AlixPartners asked 1,249 smartphone and tablet-using customers at the end of 2013 which providers they would most want to use for a digital wallet (defined as a tool that stores payment card numbers and loyalty, gift card, reward, coupon, and discount information). Close to half (46 percent) would want one from PayPal, 19 percent from Google. Half (50 percent) said they would want their primary bank to provide the service.[1]

At the same time, online microcredit and peer-to-peer lending platforms, which are also capable of eating into bank market share, have been growing and multiplying at a rapid rate. There were reportedly 33 of such platforms that were active in 2010, up from one in 2005 (the first true peer-to-peer online lending platform was Zopa). Summarized by Bachman et al. (2011),

> In this kind of lending model the mediation of financial institutions is not required ... P2P lending is a way to receive a loan without a financial institution involved in the decision process and might also be a possibility to receive better conditions than in the traditional banking system.[2]

In 2012 the peer-to-peer online lending industry volume was over $50 million in new loans per month, and in mid-2012 total loan volume passed the $1 billion mark.[3] At what level of volume and transaction size, or at what expansion of transactor scope, might these platforms be in a position to seriously encroach upon traditional financial institutions? And more to the point, what things are these traditional institutions *not* doing today that is helping to foster the growth of these financial services alternatives?

It is a somewhat puzzling irony that in the financial services sector, corporate leaders who are otherwise bold and self-confident, and whose success is founded on their ability to make daring, large, long-range decisions for the firm seem all too often unable or unwilling to make similarly bold and similarly important decisions about how their firm's information processing assets are designed, deployed, and utilized. Antiquated and patchwork data systems, along with obsolete and feature-starved process applications, can seriously undermine the competitive position of a financial institution. In many cases in which bold, long-range planning decisions are desperately needed, institutions fail to prioritize major improvements to their information processing capabilities, and this failure to prioritize can be the primary constraint on progress toward a more holistic and capable information processing infrastructure. Evidently, as we will argue, in this industry so dependent on superior information processing, institutions seem to be weak in assessing where the current investment trade-offs are, where they are headed, and how fast they are changing. One symptom of this state of affairs is the enormous difficulty and expense that firms have experienced in trying to meet post-crisis regulatory requirements, such as Comprehensive Capital Analysis and Review (CCAR). Replacing antiquated legacy capabilities and taking a more deliberate and holistic approach to information processing means not only restructuring or replacing physical data processing and analytic resources, it also means creating an organizational structure to match that modernized business model. This means that the overall strategic direction must be identified, that the underlying physical infrastructure must be aligned with that vision, and that a plan to match personnel with that model must be developed and communicated throughout the organization.

This book seeks to provide context, as well as analytic and anecdotal support, for the simple characterization described above—that to be more successful and more competitive, financial institutions need to focus on information processing as *the* core competency. It seeks to provide some organization and definitions of terms and ideas embedded in the concept of management of information assets, primarily surrounding data and information processing and statistical modeling. The goal of this exercise is to make the relationship between firm organization around these functions and overall firm strategy and performance more stark. Finally, the book provides practical observations about how information assets can be actively and effectively managed to create competitive advantage and improved financial results. Toward the end of the book we survey some case studies that highlight some of the positive and less positive results that have stemmed from institutions either recognizing or failing to recognize the strategic importance of information processing capabilities.

NOTES

1. Penny Crosman, "How Banks Can Win Back 'Mind Share' from PayPal, Google, Amazon," *American Banker*, May 30, 2014, 10.

2. Alexander Bachman, Alexander Becker, Daniel Buerkner, Michael Hilker, Frank Kock, Mark Lehmann, and Phillip Tiburtius, "Online Peer-to-Peer Lending—A Literature Review," *Journal of Internet Banking and Commerce* 16, no. 2 (August 2011).

3. Peter Renton, "Peer-to-Peer Lending Crosses $1 Billion in Loans Issued," TechCrunch (website), May 29, 2012, http://techcrunch.com/2012/05/29/peer-to-peer-lending-crosses-1-billion-in-loans-issued.

Acknowledgments

Those who deserve special thanks include Brian Peters, Karen Schneck, Andrew Clyne, Mark Almeida, Hsiu-Mei Chang, and Gordon Cooper for various contributions, edits, and moral support; Jorge Sobehart for teaching me about information entropy and many other things; and to all my wonderful and brilliant colleagues at AIG. And to Sarah Kate Venison who provided encouragement all along the way. The multitude of remaining errors and defects are of course my own.

CHAPTER 1

Financial Institutions as Information Processors

FINANCIAL INSTITUTIONS' RAISON D'ÊTRE

Economic literature includes a rich debate on why firms exist as they do—the main question being why firm boundaries are defined in the ways that we observe. Certain types of activities that could remain in-house are routinely outsourced, while many activities with the potential to be outsourced remain internal to the firm. Mergers, acquisitions, and divestitures do exhibit certain patterns with respect to how firms believe their own boundaries ought to be defined, but these patterns are by no means exhaustive nor are their outcomes obviously probative. Some corporate restructurings are metamorphic and highlight the question of what makes a financial institution a financial institution. For example, in 1987 Greyhound Corp., a bus line company since 1929, spun off its bus line operating units so that it could "focus on its core business of financial services." To even think about which firms should be defined as belonging to the financial

1

services sector we need to have some practical mechanism or criteria for inclusion. Theoretically we could simply enumerate a comprehensive list of financial services and products, and include firms that engage in this set of activities. With a boundary so constructed, we would have an identified set of institutions to analyze. But does that boundary really exist or is it helpful even as an abstraction? Retail sales finance is one of the largest and most obvious types of boundary blurring, often occurring at the direct expense of banks and retail credit suppliers. Captive finance subsidiaries for manufacturing firms are also common and the obvious complementarity between manufacturing goods and financing their sale seems to suggest that the latter function can be effectively internalized. But while the economic incentive to encroach on the boundaries of financial services seems to be predominantly one way—that is, we have not heard of things like mortgage institutions directly engaging in home construction—no hard and fast rule seems to apply.

There are well-known cases of captive finance companies whose financial services activities grew beyond financing the parent's manufactured products—in one case so much so that the entity became a systemically significant financial institution in its own right with only remnant relationships between their financing activities and the financing of the parent's products. Are there economic principles that would allow us to explain why, and the extent to which (for example) auto sales and lease financing are or are not more thoroughly internalized within auto manufacturers? While to economists the answer is surely yes (what area of human endeavor do economists feel cannot be explained by economics?), it seems clear that management teams at financial institutions themselves do not recognize or embrace such principles. For if they believed they understood the principles that define why the financial institution exists, they would surely leverage those same principles to establish firms that function better overall.

Rather than try to tackle this broader problem head on, in this book we simply focus on the kinds of firms that dominate the financial services industry landscape: banks and insurance companies. We leave it to the reader to consider whether or not the observations made also apply to any specific firm or subset of firms with financial sector exposure or activities. A number of factors characterize the financial services industry in a way that might help us better understand why financial institutions exist in the way they do, and how they can improve their economic strength and competitive positions.

Low Barriers to Entry

Over the bulk of the financial industry's long history, practical barriers to entry in banking and insurance were quite high. In the modern era this was primarily due to regulatory and licensing requirements, but also due to consumer preferences for brand stability and stature. Over the past 100 years or so great banking and insurance industry firms were founded on brand strength, and their ability to attract depositors and policy holders was their primary determinant of growth. However, those barriers began to erode during the twentieth century as cultural changes and an increasing dependence on technology changed both the supply and demand sides of financial services markets. Changing regulatory requirements produced periods that alternated between stimulating and dampening bank and insurance company formation as well as merger activity, which is beyond the scope of this book to either document or survey. What is important is that evidence can be presented to support the claim of low barriers to entry.

Interestingly, the aggregate data does not show an upward trend in the number of operating financial institutions. For banks, the total number of operating institutions in the United States hovered around 14,000 for the nearly 20 years between the early 1960s and the early 1980s. Then, after the savings and loan crisis began to unfold, the total number of banks began to drop—a trend that continues to this day, with the number of banks dropping by more than 50 percent from its 1980s total to fewer than 6,000 in 2013 (see Figure 1.1). However, looking only at the total number of institutions does not tell the whole story. In particular, the stability of the total number of institutions during that 20-year period between the 1960s and the 1980s reflected an offset between periods of great consolidation through mergers and acquisitions that reduced the total and periods of rapid entry of new institutions—particularly savings and loans associations, prior to the S&L crisis. Overall, entry into the banking sector has remained brisk and steady, despite the stable, then declining, count totals. Hubert

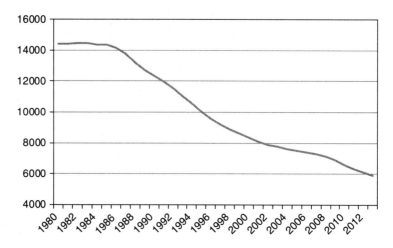

Figure 1.1 Total Commercial Banks in the United States
Source: Federal Reserve Economic Data (FRED); Federal Reserve Bank of St. Louis.

Janicki and Edward Prescott observed that, "Despite the large number of banks that have exited the industry over the last 45 years, there has been a consistent flow of new bank entries," and calculated the average annual entry rate at about 1.5 percent of operating banks. The authors further observe that, "It is striking that despite the huge number of bank exits starting in the 1980s, entry remained strong throughout the entire period. Interestingly, it is virtually uncorrelated with exit. For example, the correlation between exit and entry for the 1985–2005 period is only –0.07."[1]

Technical Core Products and Services Offered (Financial Intermediation and Disintermediation and Risk Pooling)

Janicki and Prescott also observe how market share can shift dramatically. They note that of the top ten banks in 1960 (by asset size), only three are still in the top ten.

Part of this is due to M&A (mergers and acquisitions) activity. But part of it reflects the fact that the product and service sets, based on intermediation and disintermediation and risk pooling, are technical in nature, and as trends in the underlying technologies change, firms have a great opportunity to innovate effectively and gain market share, or fail to innovate effectively and lose market share. What Figure 1.1 does show clearly is that while barriers to entry may be low, barriers to exit are even lower. Failure to stay abreast of technological innovations, as well as the adoption of so-called innovations that misrepresent true risk-adjusted returns, has been causing the number of operating banks to shrink by about 280 per year since 1984. Some of the innovations that led to distorted risk assessments include mortgage-backed securities and complex, illiquid types of derivatives (there are others). But while distorted risk assessments have historically been blamed on personal mismanagement and a culture of greed, these explanations offer little in the way of economic underpinnings and cannot explain the disappearance of nearly 8,600 banks over a 30-year period. The main culprit is that decision makers within these firms have been provided with poor information, insufficient information, and, in many cases, misinformation, and the main cause for this is that these firms were manifestly poor at information management and creation. While the S&L crisis triggered the largest number of bank closures, the bursting of the tech and housing bubbles, and the ensuing liquidity crisis of 2008, also forced many institutions to close. And in far more cases, institutions that did not fail saw their profitability greatly reduced by inefficiencies, losses, and fines—most of which could have been avoided with the appropriate amount of investment in system architecture and process redesign. Recent examples of significant regulatory fines related to information processing failures include:

- $25 billion: Wells Fargo, JPMorgan Chase, Citigroup, Bank of America, Ally Financial (2012)
- $13 billion: JPMorgan Chase (2013)
- $9.3 billion: Bank of America, Wells Fargo, JPMorgan Chase, and 10 others (2013)
- $8.5 billion: Bank of America (June 2011)
- $2.6 billion: Credit Suisse (May 2014)
- $1.9 billion: HSBC (2012)
- $1.5 billion: UBS (2012)

Taken together, these historical facts show how even very large financial institutions can suffer or even cease to exist if they fail to embrace technological innovation, or embrace it without a commensurate investment in the information management capability required to effectively evaluate risk. Thus, the stylized facts that should concern current financial institutions are:

- Firms entering the market, particularly those entering with some technological advantage, are a threat.

- Excessive risk taking based on impaired risk assessments (often the result of technological innovation without the supporting information flow) is a threat.

- The likelihood that any firm succumbing to these threats will be expelled from the market is high.

Poor information management itself has causes. In some cases, the underlying causes may have included a regulatory (and rating agency) arbitrage in which financial institutions were incented to do the minimum while benefiting from things like deposit insurance (an explicit stamp of approval from regulatory authorities) and high public ratings from rating agencies, or even the implicit stamp of approval that comes purely from compliance and the absence of regulatory censure. But more importantly and more generally, low industry standards for excellence in information processing have meant the absence of competitive pressures to innovate and excel. This environment, which has persisted for decades, is now coming to an end.

CULTURAL ISSUES

While identifying more effective management of information assets as a key strategic objective for the firm is a good first step, implementing an effective strategic management process is not without challenges within a modern financial institution. Among those are serious cultural and organizational challenges that can work against the development and deployment of an integrated approach to information management. One such challenge is so pervasive and so constraining that it deserves special consideration. Within the broader fabric of corporate culture, there lies a deep cultural rift—a rift that may be more or less pronounced depending on the business mix and particular firm characteristics, but that is almost always material. It is the rift between IT (alternately management information systems, or MIS) and non-IT. This rift has developed over decades, with rapid technological change and exponentially increasing business dependencies on technology as the driving forces. Importantly, the initials IT stand for information technology—something that should be a core competency for a financial institution. But far from being core from an integrated strategic management perspective, business managers and their IT counterparts are often separated culturally to such an extent that they are speaking different languages, both euphemistically and literally. Business executives frequently view their IT organizations with distrust. Common complaints are that their process requirements are opaque, that they do not understand the organization's business objectives, or, worst of all, that they are not motivated by incentives that are aligned with the business strategy.[2] On the other side, IT personnel often hold a dim view of the non-IT businessperson's understanding of technology generally, and IT technology in particular. The IT presumption that the business side doesn't understand its own problem, doesn't understand what the solution should be, or simply can't express itself intelligibly, can easily lead to ill-formed plans and projects whose poor outcomes further the distrust, in addition to sapping the resources of the firm. Importantly, the rift reflects the fact that information processing is not viewed as a true core competency within most financial institutions, and that consequently IT is seen as a supporting, or enabling, function—critical yes, but no more so than operating an effective health benefits program (or company cafeteria, for that matter).

The Senior Leadership Component

Senior leadership positions such as chief financial officer or chief credit officer are typically viewed not only as great executives but also as repositories of subject matter expertise and corporate history. The people who hold such positions are expected to understand the entire fabric of their respective organizations thoroughly and often are expected to have personal experience at multiple levels of job seniority. Chief credit officers will invariably have had deep experience in underwriting and workouts over a range of products and markets. Chief financial officers will usually have had deep hands-on experience in preparing and analyzing financial statements, and frequently in auditing financial accounts from different parts of the company. Unfortunately, this deep experience in their respective disciplines is a double-edged sword. As the needs within risk and finance become increasingly dependent on analytics and information processing, these leaders may not have the experience or vision to help shape the data and analytic infrastructure of the firm to enable competitive capabilities to be developed in these key areas.

Contrast this with the chief information officer, chief technology officer, or whatever the C-level executive responsible for IT is called. These leaders *are* responsible for establishing a forward-looking competitive infrastructure design and overall vision for the firm, and because their peer-level leaders may not have comparable technical depth, that responsibility may be very highly concentrated. As individuals, they have frequently distinguished themselves in general manager roles or within a specific discipline *other than IT*. But even for those with relatively deep or long-tenured association with IT, how many in the financial services industry actually rose up from within the IT culture? How many have ever personally designed a software application and seen it through each phase of the development process? How many have personally developed a major data processing system? How many have written a single line of production code? Certainly, outside the financial services industry—and not just in the technology space—the answer to all these questions would be: the majority. However, the honest answer within the financial services industry has to be: very few. This shows both the general lack of interest senior managers have in actively managing their companies as *information processing companies*, and the reason that financial institutions are so challenged by the basic needs and competitive demands that they currently face in this area.

For corporate leaders not directly responsible for IT, the acceleration of technological change within their respective disciplines has been more recent but the vintage effect of the experience base is no less pronounced. For example, 10 years ago almost all chief compliance officers were attorneys and most reported to the general counsel. As compliance risks and regulatory attention evolved toward more systemic information-based areas such as anti-money laundering (AML), customer identification programs (CIP), reporting covered under the Bank Secrecy Act of 1970 (BSA), and other types of fraud detection, more technical, risk-related training has become increasingly important. Within the AML space (now a front-burner issue, especially for larger institutions), detection solutions are increasingly based on sophisticated statistical modeling and voluminous data processing. Top-vendor AML systems deploy sophisticated models that require not only expert management and independent validation, but also rich and timely data flows that can test the capability of the institution's overall data infrastructure. Even CIP, formerly a rule-based exercise with a tendency toward weak performance measurement, continues to evolve in this direction. The Patriot Act clarification on CIP includes this statement:

> The Agencies wish to emphasize that a bank's CIP must include risk-based procedures for verifying the identity of each customer to the extent reasonable and practicable. It is critical that each bank develop procedures to account for all relevant risks including those presented by the types of accounts maintained by the bank, the various methods of opening accounts provided, the type of identifying information available, and the bank's size, location, and type of business or customer base. Thus, specific minimum requirements in the rule, such as the four basic types of information to be obtained from each customer, should be supplemented by risk-based verification procedures, where appropriate, to ensure that the bank has a reasonable belief that it knows each customer's identity.[3]

To summarize, regulators now expect financial institutions to bear the full weight of modern data management and creative, advanced analytics in addressing issues for which compliance had traditionally been a matter of minimally following highly prescriptive rule sets. Given the emphasis on risk-based techniques requiring advanced, industrial strength data processing support, chief risk officers and chief compliance officers will be challenged to lead these efforts without a technical risk-analytics and IT-oriented experience base.

Outsourcing and the Culture of Failure

Unfortunately for many firms, the problem of an inadequate experience base is self-reinforcing. How many stories have we heard about giant IT projects that were catastrophic failures? Without adequately experienced leaders in place (who could potentially prevent some of these disasters), it can be extremely difficult to get accurate assessments of why the projects failed or what could have been done better. The experience deficit has also created an information asymmetry in which business decision makers, often not completely clear about what their current and future needs are and scarred by past IT project failures, are squared off against software vendors who are often very well informed about the firm's knowledge, current capabilities, and history, and can tailor their sales pitches accordingly. Ironically, many large-scale IT failures occurred because the projects weren't nearly large enough—that is, as big as they may have been, they weren't part of a holistic redesign of the overall information processing infrastructure of the firm. At the same time, many IT-related outsourcing relationships have helped financial institutions improve performance and efficiency, creating a tremendously appealing perception that more outsourcing is better, and that financial institutions need to get out of the information processing business. But as we will discuss in more detail below, institutions need to consider carefully what aspects of their information-process complex are truly core to their identities and competitive positions in the marketplace, and invest in and further develop these internal capabilities instead of outsourcing them.

Outsourcing issues aside, all IT infrastructure projects expose the firm to some risk. In the absence of a clearly communicated overall vision, the risks associated with piecemeal infrastructure projects are elevated for a number of reasons. In the first place, even well-meaning and experienced project managers are at an informational disadvantage. They are solving *a* problem—or a narrow set of problems—without knowing whether the design choice will be complementary to other software and system projects also underway. The only way to insure strong complementarity of such projects is to have a clearly articulated vision for the overall system and to evaluate each project for consistency with that vision. For many large institutions, particularly those who have grown by acquisition, the underlying system is effectively a hodgepodge, and there may be no clearly articulated vision. Under these conditions, the chance that any one project will make the problem worse is high. This can lead decision makers to embrace min-max strategies[4] with respect to high-visibility infrastructure projects—often strategies that can be supported with information from industry experts, including consultants and the software vendors themselves, who certainly do not have a long-term vision for the firm's competitive position as a goal. In many cases, both the requirements for a given infrastructure build and the design choices made in order to meet those requirements are partly or wholly outsourced to vendors, consultants, or both. From asset/liability management systems, to Basel II/III systems, to AML systems, to model governance systems, to general purpose database and data processing systems, key expertise and decision making are routinely outsourced. Recognizing this, the sales presentations from the major software firms increasingly involve selling the vendor-as-expert, not just the product. Consulting firms, too, have increasingly oriented their marketing strategies toward this approach under the (frequently correct) assumption that the audience is operating on the short end of an information asymmetry, understanding primarily that it has a *problem* and needs a *solution*. Vendors' increasing focus on integrated solutions reflects their perception that institutions are now aware that they have bigger problems and are increasingly willing to outsource the vision for how the firm manages its analytic assets in the broadest sense.

The outsourcing approach can be expedient, particularly when an institution does not have the immediately required technical knowledge. And since design choices require both technical/product knowledge and a deep understanding of the particular institutional needs and constraints (and history), adding internal expertise through hiring may not be a quick solution either, since new hires may know less than consultants about the internal workings of a given firm. But such knowledge and expertise gaps may be symptoms of a deeper underlying problem and, particularly when regulatory expectations are involved, the persistence of the expertise gaps that led to the outsourcing can come back to haunt the firm. One illustrative example is that of AML. At many banks, sophisticated vendor-provided transaction-monitoring software is used for AML alert processes. In fact, the sophistication of these systems has been increasing rapidly over the past several years, to the delight of institutions that see these systems as solving a real problem caused by increasing expectations of regulators. But both the understanding of how these systems work and the back-testing and tuning of the many settings required to operationalize them have, in many cases, been outsourced to the vendors who supply the product. Predictably, regulators who applaud the installation of such capable technology have been highly critical of the banks' actual deployment of it. Generally, negative feedback from the regulators about the implementation of these systems has included the following complaints:

- The company is not using the full functionality of the system.
- The system is not adequately customized to align with the company's risk profile.
- The program does not capture all of the company's products and services.
- The scenarios or rules used do not adequately cover the company's risks.
- There are no statistically valid processes in place to evaluate the automated transaction monitoring system.
- There are insufficient MIS and metrics to manage and optimize the system.

More recently, the Fed has issued explicit statements that it considers such systems to be models and that therefore the requirements of SR 11-7[5] apply—requirements that few compliance teams or model validation teams are fully prepared to meet. Clearly, the regulatory community is quite sensitive to the fact that outsourced solutions without close internal expertise and oversight may be ineffective in achieving their goals, and in the AML area this sensitivity is backed up by firsthand experience obtained in the course of examinations. But AML is just one example. And regulators' concerns aside, the firms themselves should be very sensitive to these same issues. For any large information processing project for which a significant amount of planning, design specification, vendor selection, implementation, tuning or validation is outsourced, the ability of the firm to maximize the value of the resulting system will be compromised. If we adhere to the view that a firm's competitive advantage will derive largely from the relative effectiveness of the management of the broad range of information assets, then the outsourcing of the vision itself to a software vendor who is marketing that same vision to other institutions amounts to nothing less than a decision to make the firm less competitive.

It is not obvious how an institution should approach narrowing or eliminating the IT rift, but one thing is clear: It needs to be recognized by the senior leaders of the firm as a challenge to be overcome, and this is unlikely to occur unless corporate leaders themselves are more IT savvy than they have been historically. A more deliberate and holistic approach to information processing means not only structuring physical data processing and analytic capabilities (as discussed below), it also means creating an organizational structure to match that modernized business model (also discussed below). This means that the overall strategic direction must be identified, that the underlying physical infrastructure must be aligned with that vision, and that a plan to match personnel with that model must be developed and communicated throughout the organization. One of the principle consumers of that communication has to be the firm's human resources department, which may itself be required to take transformative steps in order to implement that strategy. The existence of dedicated IT HR departments that only hire into IT roles serves to propagate and reinforce the rift. (Interestingly, poll data from users of internal service providers within U.S. corporations found satisfaction rates for IT (MIS) and HR at 28 and 24 percent respectively[6]—dead last among internal providers.) If the HR function does not clearly understand the need for more strategically deployed skill sets across functions and across the revamped information processing complex, it will be impossible to implement such a strategy. This means more subject matter experts need to be embedded directly into the HR organization.

IT LITERACY AND THE SPREADSHEET DELUGE

Interestingly, the cultural IT rift that is often systemic within an institution is preserved across a wide array of different business processes and sub-entities, even though the constituents have widely varying interests, objectives, and technical expertise. For example, line personnel and process managers may view IT through the lens of laptops, email, portable devices, and the like. Traders may see IT through the lens of complex trading system implementations and sophisticated asset valuation models. Finance teams may rely heavily on stable and long-standing ledger systems and view IT purely as a so-called keep-the-lights-on function. Process owners looking for application development often see the IT team as the project management wildcard, unable to be controlled through the tools the process owners typically use to manage every other aspect of a given project. However, throughout the financial services industry the main boundary that divides the realm of the IT constituents from the non-IT constituents is the Excel spreadsheet. More broadly, using the current lexicon, the latter is the realm of the end-user tool (EUT). EUTs are defined in just that way—they are not controlled by or interfered with by IT. The end user may create, populate, alter, rename, copy, share, and email the EUT at will. Importantly, because spreadsheets and supported processes live outside the sphere of formal IT control, the control practices and capabilities used within IT organizations to control production-level systems and processes are usually unavailable to help with EUT control. These include robust documentation requirements, including signed-off specification documents, restricted access and version control, user acceptance testing (UAT), and back-up and business continuity requirements.

In many institutions, the cost of controllership for spreadsheet-based processes has historically been close to zero. Spreadsheets could be developed without any of the onerous involvement of IT, and with virtually no requirements for documentation, independent validation, access and version control, or other operational risk mitigants. In this zero-cost environment, the use of spreadsheets exploded. On the positive side, the dominance of spreadsheet-based analytics has led to a highly agile environment in which business functions can quickly meet their own analytic needs using spreadsheets (often needs that are rapidly changing), at low cost. However, the unfortunate effect of this freedom is that key processes that any institution would want to have some level of controllership over are too frequently managed largely or entirely through EUTs. In such cases data storage, data processing, modeling, and reporting may all be performed through EUTs. When inefficient tools are used for data storage and data processing, the institution loses information creation capacity and can lose information outright or create misinformation. When spreadsheets are used as data repositories the situation is somewhat worse. If a spreadsheet is storing unique data and information, that data or information will be available to only those few users who have access to and full understanding of the spreadsheet. Thus, the data or information embedded in the spreadsheet has been housed in an institutional dead end. If the spreadsheet is storing redundant data or information, then it is simply creating an unnecessary controllership cost and operational risk. This is typically the case, since data within a financial institution rarely originates from an EUT. In considering the efficiency of its information processing complex, an institution can consider this simple rule of thumb: *End-user tools should be handling end uses only.* They belong in what we will refer to as the analytic layer.

Demands on financial institutions for better information processing controls are changing the landscape for EUT use. This has largely been spurred by regulators, who have been put in the position of examining risk and financial reporting processes managed largely through webs of nested spreadsheets. Their demands for transparency, documentation, and effective control often prove difficult to meet. Physical control of a known and fixed set of EUTs, and especially spreadsheets, is becoming somewhat easier as vendor-provided spreadsheet-control systems are becoming more capable and more user-friendly. Such systems provide audit trails covering file use, access, change control monitoring, and other diagnostics. But the actual cost of controlling spreadsheet-based processes is often inflated because of the cost of reducing the process to a known and fixed set of EUTs and of documenting the design and purpose of each such process. Just tracing through the path of the data is challenging when the process is composed of complex systems of nested and linked spreadsheets, augmented by myriad cuttings and pastings of data from one to another. With such processes being difficult to even diagram, and the boundaries of the process difficult to establish, adding control capabilities to a subset of key EUTs may provide very little controllership to the process overall.

From the perspective of knowledge and experience, a *crowding-out effect* is clearly evident across the financial services industry: The higher the demand for spreadsheet-expert analysts, the narrower the flow of training and expertise in alternate technologies. Part of this has been the result of the successful strategy of Microsoft to promote spreadsheet use for a wider and wider array of uses, which comes at the expense of a more segmented approach to data management and analysis. In the 1980s as the PC boom began in earnest, sophisticated yet user-friendly database tools also took off, spearheaded by products like FoxPro and Ashton-Tate's dBase. These tools integrated a basic SQL (Structured Query Language) type of functionality with FORTRAN-based programming languages and could be managed by business experts looking to solve applied business problems as opposed to computer scientists. Microsoft sought to redirect attention away from these do-it-yourself applications, releasing its middle-ground Access product and acquiring (and then discontinuing) the feature-rich FoxPro. These market tactics altered the flow of experience accumulation and helped to create the IT rift. Short-term trade-offs became the rule for business executives who were faced with accomplishing tasks under time pressure and who had no direct personal stake in the institution's overall information processing architecture, creating stronger and stronger incentives to extend the breadth and depth of spreadsheet use and to continue to accumulate spreadsheet-analytic skills in their respective teams.

These days an experienced spreadsheet expert can be deployed and redeployed cross-functionally with a very low ramp-up cost. Alternatively, any consideration of a non-spreadsheet-based solution to a process that is currently spreadsheet-based means the involvement of IT personnel, who will not likely be viewed as subject matter experts or as expeditors. As a result, the manager can economize on difficult-to-manage IT resources, bulk up on subject matter expertise, and retain control of his time line by keeping the analytic and reporting functions of his group spreadsheet-based. This trend has further insulated business analytics teams from IT personnel and policies, and further isolated the IT teams from a wide array of business-critical processes. And because of this isolation effect, IT personnel who could potentially engineer more efficient alternatives to the spreadsheet deluge, or at least help to manage the risks and complexities that stem from the overuse of spreadsheets, are not even fully aware of the problem or which processes are being impacted. Without the perspective of more technology savvy personnel who also understand the business processes, out-of-control spreadsheet processes can appear insoluble.

Consider the following example: a project to consolidate various data sources relevant for risk modeling within a large financial institution—a project designed partly to streamline reporting capabilities, but primarily to streamline and improve controllership for analytics teams building statistical models within divisional business units (an important SR11-7 component). The largest business unit team, a thirty-some person team that included multiple PhDs and other modeling experts, was decidedly unenthusiastic after sitting through the initial training demo. "But how do we actually get the data out?" the team members asked. "Through SQL queries," the project managers answered. "The data is organized to make the queries really intuitive and straightforward." The analytics team was shown a simple, user-friendly query window and given a demonstration of the power and performance of the system. "But no one on our team knows SQL," the group complained. Undaunted by this surprising revelation from such a technical group, the project managers countered, "That's okay, you can link to the tables using Microsoft Access; use that interface and you'll see hardly any decrease in performance." "But no one on our team knows Access either," the team members said, "we only use Excel."

By contrast, consider the working operating model at Loan Pricing Corporation, a small bank services company that operated independently during the 1990s and was later acquired. This company was effectively providing outsourcing of portfolio analytics and statistical modeling for commercial banks, with the benefit of having access to data from multiple banks (confidentially supplied) to support those work streams. One of the things that made this small company exceptional was that the entire bank database (a simple but large relational database implemented in Sybase) was made available to every employee involved in analytic work, and each one of these employees was required to be fully self-sufficient with respect to the access and use of that data. SQL was the lingua franca at the firm, with the effect that data-supported processes were extremely direct and highly efficient, and a wide variety of operational risks were effectively mitigated. On the other hand, the operational risk associated with incorrect query writing was proportionally elevated. However, the culture of the firm was dramatically and positively shaped by the requirement that analysts know SQL and access data directly from the central database. First, the level of SQL expertise—and the consequent understanding of the data itself—was driven to high levels, as each employee's neighbor on the right and the left was highly capable and the competitive pressure to be expert in query writing was therefore palpable. Second, due to the direct pulling of data by the analysts themselves, the level of scrutiny and of data profiling was raised far beyond what typically exists in banks, with the result that data cleansing became an indirect ancillary service supplied to client banks. This superior outsourcing of data cleansing enhanced the credibility of the models being produced, and the quality of other analytic services was also enhanced in the eyes of the clients. Last, the importance placed on skill with SQL and data processing had a powerful democratizing effect on the culture of the company, eliminating the IT rift and providing a separate mechanism to support a meritocracy in work assignments and promotions. While the company changed hands more than once and its performance was buffeted by a variety of broader trends, many alumni from this firm went on to positions in the financial services industry through which they influenced and advanced the information processing capabilities of their subsequent employers.

As regulatory requirements for information processing control have increased, spearheaded in part by the Federal Reserve Bank's CCAR process,[7] the need for financial institutions to better understand and control their EUT use has increased. For most institutions, just knowing what EUTs it has, what they are used for, and where they are located is a major challenge. Several software vendors now offer tools capable of searching through corporate networks to identify and count EUTs, and in some cases to provide varying levels of analysis of the EUTs identified. Anecdotal accounts hold that even medium-sized banks have tens of millions of EUTs extant on their corporate networks. Presumably millions more exist on local drives, inaccessible to network-crawling tools. One vendor recounted an experience with a global bank based in Europe that (due to system constraints) was only able to perform a network scan on its home country corporate network, where it discovered 31 million EUTs—of which more than half had not been accessed in more than a year. Clearly, the accumulation of such large numbers of spreadsheets creates multiple forms of cost for the institution. These costs include:

- Loss of information, as the origins of the data become murky and the results can no longer be relied upon or attested to.

- Replication, as the loss of knowledge about the nature and purpose of a given spreadsheet creates the need to recreate something identical (or nearly identical).

- Operational risk, as the certainty that a given spreadsheet is fit for its intended purpose will degrade over time and the potential for the spreadsheet to become corrupted or simply outdated will grow over time.

- Physical resource drag, as the memory consumption alone from tens of millions of spreadsheets, many of which no longer have any useful purpose, reduces the capacity and can impair the performance of existing hardware.

- Compliance costs, as internal or external demands for documentation, or for minimal forms of controllership, become increasingly difficult and costly to comply with.

Spreadsheet control, and more broadly EUT control, is one of the current hot topics in financial institution risk management circles, and regulators are now demanding that institutions have comprehensive EUT control capabilities in place in order to clear other regulatory hurdles such as SOX (the 2002 Sarbanes-Oxley Act) and CCAR exams.

OTHER CHALLENGES TO ESTABLISHING AN IT-SAVVY CULTURE

Beyond the challenges imposed by the IT rift and the technical knowledge gap typical within management and HR functions, understanding and managing large financial institutions as a unique class of firms has additional cultural complexities. These stem from the fact that financial institutions are typically composed of multiple, highly heterogeneous product and service lines, with a strong correlation between firm size and the heterogeneity of these activities. This gives rise to a tendency toward localized solutions, and frustrates the centralization of data and information processing that would give rise to economies of scale and enable the establishment of an integrated and consistent vision for information processing.

Frequently, constituents engaged in certain sets of activities will try to segregate themselves from the firm's efforts to develop an integrated and efficient information management framework (and culture). These may be the within-firm leaders in information processing, in which case the talent and experience of the individuals involved and the capabilities of the system architecture should be tapped by HQ leaders to help shape the corporate vision. Other groups may be Luddites culturally, unwilling to accept that their business practices could be improved through better information management and use, with antiquated practices that can create a drag on local and firm-wide competitiveness as well as creating unnecessary operational risk.

In large institutions, the best run *data* processing business units are typically in the retail banking, transaction services, and consumer credit spaces. All of these are very high data volume businesses with industry-level transactions numbering in the hundreds of billions per year and continuing to grow rapidly. But even in areas like transaction banking, where financial institutions are doing the best job relative to other internal departments, they are in fact only tenuously in possession of a technological advantage at the industry level and are quite vulnerable to threats from more capable firms outside of or on the fringe of the financial services sector. Illustrating that vulnerability (and as mentioned in the introduction), the *Wall Street Journal* reported in April of 2014 that Wal-Mart:

> aims to take a bite out of the roughly $900 billion in
> so-called person-to-person payments made each year in
> the U.S., in the form of cash or checks ... The new service
> brings Wal-Mart even deeper into the of providing
> traditional banking services even though the company
> isn't technically a bank.[8]

For true strength in information processing within the financial services sector, consumer credit product providers tend to be among the best. These businesses, which include consumer credit card, mortgage, personal loan, and other small ticket financings, combine proficiency in high transaction volume data processing with cutting-edge model-based *information* processing technologies. Extending and monitoring credit for what can easily number in the tens of millions of accounts at a large institution requires superior data management and information processing on a number of fronts. On the analytics side, most of the heavy lifting in consumer credit businesses is performed by sophisticated credit scoring models, as well as marketing, line-limit adjustment, and fraud detection models for which what is defined as state of the art changes almost quarterly. While historically these businesses outsourced credit scoring to the primary credit bureaus, competitive pressures have driven them toward more sophisticated proprietary models that use bureau scores as one type of input. Importantly, these proprietary systems need to maintain the nearly instantaneous response time that the bureaus provide or customer acquisition rates can suffer. However, in spite of the expertise and physical information processing capabilities contained within these businesses, they are all too often closely held within the business lines themselves and not integrated into the overall information processing design of the institution. In most cases, this is simply because the institution isn't taking an integrated, cross-product approach to system design. In part, this may stem from managers' beliefs that only the consumer credit and consumer insurance businesses are high data-volume businesses and that it does not make sense to combine these with relatively low data-volume commercial business lines. But as we will discuss further in Chapter 2, the volumes of data that can, and ultimately must be, brought to bear to create competitive commercial financial institutions are (and will be) so high that such a distinction no longer makes sense as a system design principle.

Even within the so-called consumer side of the house, integration often takes a back seat to the product view of organizational segmentation. For example, it is typical for banks with multiple credit card programs, sales finance programs, and personal loan, auto loan, and mortgage loans, to store and model the key information related to these exposures at the *account* level, rather than at the *customer* level. This is ironic given that the most powerful and widely used inputs into these models are other models—namely the consumer bureau credit scores—that are developed and applied at the *customer* level. The irony is exacerbated by the fact that the identifiers for these bureau scores are social security numbers, individual taxpayer IDs, or both, which is precisely the information needed to integrate the consumer data at the customer level. And while the types of consumer data that can be collected and used for modeling are governed by a host of regulations,[9] certainly the amount of information that could be generated or collected to improve the assessment of creditworthiness and the effectiveness of marketing efforts is not anywhere near the maximum. Now, powerful regulatory pressures are forcing firms to adopt more customer-centric information processing capabilities. New and higher standards for the production of suspicious activity reports (SARs) required under the Bank Secrecy Act are effectively requiring banks to apply new SARs-alert algorithms at the customer level, and this is causing many firms to radically remediate or replace their account-based data models.

By contrast, large commercial operations and certain capital market activities retain some of the most antiquated thinking about data, information processing, and analytics. The most obvious evidence of this is the continued heavy use of agency ratings as summary statistics for credit assessment and pricing. It should not be controversial at this point to assert that deal making and the pricing of corporate credit based on the deliberately slow-moving and opaquely generated agency ratings—whose track record is fraught with errors and omissions—does not constitute maximally informed decision making. Of course, another potentially limiting aspect of this practice is the narrowness of the universe covered by the major agencies. Very often, such limitations are overcome (when driven by necessity) by extending the rated universe with so-called internal ratings, EDFs (expected default frequencies), or other substitutes without adjusting the process to account for the different types of information content contained in each. Shockingly, at many institutions there is little recognition of the fact that these different types of indicators do in fact have widely varying information content and quality, even though they are key inputs into pricing and structuring decisions, and often drive risk limits and approval authority. The connection between the quality of credit information and competitive advantage is immediate and direct, especially since institutions' practices in this area differ widely and produce widely varying outcomes—a fact that we can easily prove.

In 2009, the Financial Services Authority (FSA) repeated an exercise it had conducted in 2007 to assess the variability across institutions in assigning probabilities of default (PDs)[10]—the quantitative analogue to credit ratings. It surveyed firm-level PDs from 13 separate financial institutions. Specifically, the FSA requested firms' PDs for 50 sovereign obligors, 100 banks, and 200 corporations as of June 30, 2009. Table 1.1 reproduces Table 1 from the FSA report, showing the variance in measured PD for co-rated obligors and broken out by obligor category. Focusing on the line for corporations, one can see that while one firm saw the average default risk for 13 well-known obligors at 3.2 percent, another saw it at 18.8 percent. The rest of the table, as well as the other statistics presented in this and the prior FSA study, confirm the wide variability of PD estimates across financial institutions. The implications of this for the pricing of debt, credit default swaps, and other derivatives, as well as for the approach to marketing products and services for corporate clients are obvious. With such widely varying underlying views, these markets are clearly highly inefficient with huge profit and loss potential hanging in the balance. We may as well close the thought by tying it back to our central theme: While all of these institutions may have the PDs wrong, one of them has them the least wrong and can out-price and out-trade its peers; this firm is gaining this advantage through superior data and information processing.

As we will argue next: As a definition and general principle, unless data has accuracy characteristics that are known probabilistically, it does not even meet the criteria to be considered information. Therefore, similar measures whose probabilistic characteristics differ cannot be used interchangeably or in combination unless the characteristics of the combined or substituted information are carefully preserved. In other words, while agency ratings, EDFs, and other indicative data may all have valuable information content themselves, they may lose that

Table 1.1 FSA Co-Rated PD Variance

			PD Statistics for Sovereign, Bank, and Corporate Portfolios (co-rated sample)		
				PD (%)	
	1	2	3	4	5	6
	Respondents in Co-Rated Sample	Number of Obligors	Average Portfolio Mean	Lowest Portfolio Mean	Highest Portfolio Mean	Range
Sovereigns	10	17	1.9%	0.6%	3.1%	2.5%
Banks	13	34	5.4%	3.0%	8.6%	5.6%
Corporations	7	13	9.1%	**3.2%**	**18.8%**	**15.7%**

Source: Financial Services Authority, *Report to the G–20 Finance Ministers and Central Bank Governors* (2009). P3.

content if they are used as loose substitutes or combined willy-nilly. The question commercial lending and investing institutions should be asking if they are serious about gaining some competitive advantage in the credit space is: How much actual information can I put into my credit measures (e.g., PDs) to deliver to decision makers and at what cost?

In certain cases, business participants may eschew the value of data and the necessity of being informed by claiming to be only price takers. As such, their need for collecting and processing data, other than for the most basic reporting requirements, or for higher level analytics, or statistical modeling, is minimal to nonexistent. As we discuss further in Chapter 3, the identification of activities that can be characterized as price taking is in fact evidence of a lack of competitiveness, which is likely the result of the firm's failure to develop an integrated and efficient information management framework and culture.

NOTES

1. Hubert P. Janicki and Edward S. Prescott, "Changes in the Size Distribution of U.S. Banks: 1960–2005," *Federal Reserve Bank of Richmond Economic Quarterly* 92, no. 4 (Fall 2006): 305.
2. Richard Hays provides an excellent, if somewhat dated, description of these dynamics; see Richard D. Hays, *Internal Service Excellence: A Manager's Guide to Building World-Class Internal Service Unit Performance* (Sarasota, FL: Summit Executive Press, 1996).
3. Board of Governors of the Federal Reserve System, "FAQs: Final CIP Rule" (2005), www.federalreserve.gov/boarddocs/SRLETTERS/2005/SR0509a1.pdf.
4. Min-max strategies are intended to minimize the maximum regret, or alternatively, to narrow the range of outcomes that could be called a failure.
5. SR 11-7, the Fed's guidance on model risk management, will be discussed further in Chapter 4.
6. Hays, *Internal Service Excellence*, 19.
7. The Fed's CCAR (Comprehensive Capital Analysis and Review) assessment will be discussed further in Chapter 3.
8. Paul Ziobro and Robin Sidel, "Wal-Mart Undercuts Rivals with New U.S. Money Transfer Service," *Wall Street Journal*, April 17, 2014.
9. An example of one regulation governing the use of consumer data is Regulation B of the Federal Reserve Board's Equal Credit Opportunity Act of 1974.
10. Financial Services Authority, "Report to the G-20 Finance Ministers and Central Bank Governors" (2009).

CHAPTER **2**

Strategic Hardware and Software Management

OVERVIEW

Managing the complex and evolving suite of hardware and software that a financial institution needs to operate effectively is a somewhat daunting task. It is usually made more difficult because the overlapping vintages of legacy systems and critical process dependencies make major design changes extremely difficult. The phrase "changing the wheels on a bus while it's still driving" is often used to describe large IT system changes, and with good reason. But to the extent that financial institutions are simply unwilling to take on major system redesign projects because they are too difficult, too risky, or both, they are creating great economic opportunity for those who are willing and able. Certainly, the best motivator and greatest risk mitigant is a clear vision for what a modernized system ought to look like, and what capabilities would be created or greatly enhanced by implementing such a system. Armed with this vision, an institution can plan to advance toward that vision using a combination of opportunistic and incremental changes and larger, more deliberate transformation projects. And, equally importantly, incremental or large steps that are *inconsistent* with the vision can be avoided.

One of the biggest questions and challenges when it comes to overall system design is the level of centralization and integration that an institution should target. By centralization we mean that data is all ultimately, officially stored in one originating data model, although it may be passed down to more local and more specialized data structures to facilitate use. By integration, we mean the existence of common identifying information for like data elements across data structures. Two data structures that contain overlapping data, for which common identifiers exist in each, can be said to be integrated. If all of the overlapping data in both systems is identical and has identical identifiers, the two systems can be said to be fully integrated. One of the principle suggestions of this book is that an institution should consider this goal—the targeting of a desired level of centralization and integration of data storage—as a key strategic decision. Local (so-called) data marts whose contents include locally loaded data that did not originate from the core system, or cannot be directly tied back to the core model, lack both centralization and integration. One of the main problems with a lack of integration is that it creates the need for reconciliation, and data reconciliations are costly and create operational risk. Data emanating from an integrated data repository do not need reconciliation.

To illustrate, consider a situation in which several account management systems feed cash-flow data into a GL (general ledger) aggregated to the product-within-a-country level. Meanwhile, local systems calculate cash-flow statistics at the legal entity level. If the systems are integrated, then each cash-flow data component has a unique identifier and a common time stamp. That means that for an identified subset of the data existing in multiple physical instances in different parts of the broader system, direct consistency tests can easily be coded and fully automated. In this case, SQL-based delta functions can quickly compare two identified objects to see if they are identical and report differences where they are found. If the system is not integrated, reconciliation will typically consist of comparing the fully aggregated totals and determining whether the observed differences are within a given error tolerance. Then, if the differences exceed the tolerance level, a research project is launched in which data are incrementally dis-aggregated by product, country, and legal entity and more localized reconciliations applied. These then consist of more local subtotals com-pared against lower preset error tolerances, and local subject matter experts tasked with explaining differences that exceed tolerance lev-els, often spawning new, more localized research projects. In many large financial institutions, reconciliation is a permanent, constant, and resource-consumptive control requirement, whose scale is inversely proportional to the lack of system integration across the key functional areas of risk and finance, and between business unit and corporate level processes.

Another key design consideration is scale—how much data should the institution be prepared to store in its core system, now and in the future? As we will argue, the amount, quality, and variety of *informa-tion* that an institution can create and use is a function of the amount, quality, and variety of *data* it has at its disposal. As we will also argue, while an institution need not have data stored in its core system to have the data at its disposal, the accessibility and controllership of data contained in a core system, as well as the ease with which the data can be combined, create efficiencies not enjoined with data stored or accessed from sources outside the core system. Since the dawn of the computer age, the amount of data stored and used and the units by which computer capabilities are reckoned have grown exponentially. As shown in Table 2.1, the very terms that practitioners use to describe computer storage volume (for specific systems and in aggregate) have evolved along with this exponential growth. The world's technological capacity to store data grew from approximately 2.6 exabytes in 1986 to 15.8 in 1993, to over 54.5 in 2000, and to 295 exabytes in 2007. Today it is being reckoned in zettabytes and massive new databases are continually being created for private and commercial use. More and more of the world's activities, down to some of the most minute and trivial details, are being captured and stored (somewhere) digitally. Institutions that will rely on data-intensive information creation to sur-vive will need to have nearly unlimited capacity to acquire data that they can identify as having value in supporting that information cre-ation process. Of course, more data is better only if it can be acquired

Table 2.1 Units Used to Describe Computer Storage

Label	Power	Bytes	Description
Byte (B)	$= 1$	1	One character of text
Kilobyte (KB)	$= 10^3$	1,000	One page of text
Megabyte (MB)	$= 10^6$	1,000,000	One small photo
Gigabyte (GB)	$= 10^9$	1,000,000,000	About 10 minutes of high-definition video
Terabyte (TB)	$= 10^{12}$	1,000,000,000,000	The largest commercial hard drives
Petabyte (PB)	$= 10^{15}$	1,000,000,000,000,000	About one hour of AT&T's digital traffic on an average business day
Exabyte (EB)	$= 10^{18}$	1,000,000,000,000,000,000	100,000 times the information stored at the Library of Congress
Zettabyte (ZB)	$= 10^{21}$	1,000,000,000,000,000,000,000	One billion terabytes

without degrading system performance or creating unmanageable reconciliation requirements or other operational risks.

To develop a strategy for intelligent system design as well as efficient software procurement and deployment, it may help to break the problem down into smaller, more manageable chunks. Essentially, there are three things an institution needs to do with data, all of which require hardware and software. They are:

1. Storage and retrieval

2. Processing

3. Analytics and reporting

These three categories of activity represent truly separate and distinct functions that require different skills and training to perform and manage. However, at many institutions these functions are distributed across the firm in support of local processes, and these local processes frequently lump all three (or any two) of these together under the direction of a single manager or team. The technical dynamics (and personnel dynamics) within each of these three disciplines differ markedly. Software capabilities are wide-ranging and rapidly evolving, and products within each of these categories are often supported by separate internal product acquisition and maintenance processes. So acquiring the best tools to perform these tasks and ensuring that they are being aligned correctly with the appropriate user base, and that users are adequately trained, should be one of the top strategic objectives of the modern financial institution. But this is no simple task. Because industrial-strength data storage hardware tends to be either fungible or bundled with proprietary software, and because it is easier to evaluate system design features in terms of how well they support specific uses of data and information (as opposed to the physical features of the system), it may be easier to determine the overall system design first and treat decisions about the necessary software and hardware as dependent subsequent steps.

Each software solution will be associated with various types of internal and external dynamics that affect its efficiency and effectiveness, both as a stand-alone product and as a component of a firm's information processing infrastructure. These include technical obsolescence, the depth of the local and global experience pool, changes stemming from increasing data volumes, cross-product compatibility, look-and-feel trends, and other user expectations. These differences and dynamics need to be recognized and assessed holistically if the institution is to optimize its overall information processing capabilities. The following paragraphs briefly list and describe the most important and impactful features of each.

Storage and Retrieval

As explained above, there are three things an institution needs to do with data: store and retrieve, process, and analyze and report on it. Storage and retrieval software, hardware, and architectural design are fundamental to the efficient use of large volumes of data. Industrial strength databases are huge, complex, expensive, and costly to change. And yet overall information efficiency begins with the underlying storage and retrieval systems, so physical capabilities should drive the system design and product selection processes. In many cases, the storage and retrieval software comes bundled under the same brand as the physical database hardware. In stark contrast to the software tools devoted to data analytics and reporting, which are subject to a frothy churn of specialized tools, rapidly evolving techniques, and boom-and-bust vendors, the landscape of storage and retrieval software has been remarkably stable. It is based on scientific principles of database architecture and a theory of database design, with SQL as the basic codeveloped data moving and processing software. These have been the features of commercial data storage and retrieval virtually since the beginning, and can be traced back to Edgar F. Codd's influential 1970 paper written at IBM, "A Relational Model of Data for Large Shared Data Banks." This paper helped to establish the principles of database design that are still current today, supported now by four decades of experience. Also, since 1986 the American National Standards Institute (ANSI) has maintained standards of the SQL language that vendors are strongly incented to conform to. Importantly, because of the relative stability of core architecture design principles and operating software, institutions bear little obsolescence risk in committing to long-run core data system design strategies. It is worth noting that this pioneering research in data system design was targeted directly toward the financial services industry, as it was perceived to be the obvious commercial leader in this field—a position they can no longer claim to hold.

One of the key revelations of these pioneering researchers was that storage and retrieval performance was highly *insensitive* to data volume as long as the data was normalized. Normalization can be thought of simply as structuring the data to speed up the process of storage and retrieval, although as it turned out, other forms of data processing (besides storage and retrieval) can also be performed at very high efficiency if the data is sufficiently normalized. A fully normalized data structure might look like Table 2.2. In this case, all of a wide variety of data elements are stored in a single table. Each record has a *record ID*, which helps the computer locate specific data elements. Each record also has a *date*, which in this case is the *as of* date for the specific data point. The data itself, whatever it may be, is stored in the *value* field. Anything can be stored in this single table: corn prices, telephone numbers, baseball scores, air temperatures, and so on. Heterogeneity is not a problem and is not relevant. The *code* field is what is used to identify the data. The code itself links to a separate *look-up table* or sequence of look-up tables that identify the contents of the value field of corn prices, telephone numbers, baseball scores, air temperatures, or whatever. When the data is stored this way, the computer can retrieve a data element or a function of the data—for example, the maximum corn price—equally fast, whether there are 10,000 or 100,000,000 corn prices in the table. Thus, to efficiently store and retrieve very large amounts of data, normalization is the

Table 2.2 Example of Normalized Data

Record ID	Date	Value	Code
1000045432	12/16/1981	0.903313	A1000651
1000045433	12/16/1981	31.25695	A2225667
1000045434	12/17/1981	0.891415	H0000654
1000045435	12/17/1981	0.188663	H1000678
1000045436	12/17/1981	729.7388	KK247650
1000045437	12/18/1981	0.166078	KK247000
1000045438	12/18/1981	0.928658	KL000766
1000045439	12/18/1981	0.287077	M000032
1000045440	12/19/1981	5138.047	ZZZ76543
...	...	...	...

key. This remarkable result does have limits and limitations. Data volumes can get large enough to impair performance. As data volumes rise, the questions that institutions must answer include these: How much and what types of data should be stored in this structured way (as opposed to not being stored or not being structured)?[1] Where should consolidated normalization be applied versus distributed normalization? And, are there alternative storage and retrieval modes that could replace or augment these traditional design principles?

The big three—Oracle, Sybase, and Teradata—all support the complex but normalized data models required by complex financial institutions. All also offer proprietary logical data models designed for complex financial service providers. Each has a variety of proprietary hardware features and some idiosyncratic SQL features as a result, so compatibility across these platforms is not complete or costless. It is also apparent that huge efficiencies accrue when an institution adopts a uniform product standard across the firm. It is not our purpose here, nor is it within the expertise of the author, to evaluate the subtleties of current brand-name technologies for bulk data storage and retrieval. But a few observations may be made about how financial institutions can improve their approach to this critical infrastructure. First, an overall architecture strategy must be developed by an experienced internal owner. Second, the core relational data model must hold data in its most granular and elemental form. Third, to combine efficiency with flexibility, a telescoping data system design is needed wherein the specialization of the data model (denormalization) scales with a scaled structure of use and user. Last, the design should not be based on the limitations of the account and other systems from which the majority of the internal data are sourced, but from a view of how these source systems *ought to work,* along with a plan for how these systems can be improved over time.

Cloud storage and other outsourced storage solutions may or may not be consistent with the centralized integrated model, depending on the need to restructure the data to conform to the requirements of the host. The distributed nature of cloud-stored data appears to create certain constraints that could degrade the desired performance properties of the core system unless that system was designed from inception as a distributed storage model.[2] However, this is a rapidly evolving set of technologies, so it is important to keep an open mind about how they may contribute, now and in the future. To set such a target, it is obviously necessary to carefully consider the core functionality of the system, and identify (categorically) the data elements required to support that functionality, identifying at the same time data and functionality that could be considered noncore and could be managed through an architecture that is outside or ancillary to the core system architecture.

Data Processing

Data processing simply means performing a set of fixed calculations and manipulations on a fixed, often large set of data, or simply moving data from one place to another. Pure data processing software and servicing as a product set has waned somewhat in importance since its heyday in the 1970s and 1980s, as it has seen encroachment from both the storage and retrieval side and from the analytics and reporting side, and as it has evolved as a specialized set of services. The industry has a long history of coming to market as a service, providing outsourced solutions for payroll, accounts receivable, and accounts payable management, and for smaller firms, general ledger and tax accounting services. In the early days, banks would store data on internal mainframe systems, pump out raw data to the data processor, and receive processed data in return. The data processors' possession of large mainframe computers with excess capacity (as well as programming expertise) established their niche. With improvements in technology, financial institutions have trended toward managing more of their own GL and tax processing internally, and outsourcing of data processing has evolved toward a few key, high-volume activities such as payroll, purchasing and receiving, so-called enterprise resource planning (ERP), and the management of customer and marketing data, commonly known as customer and relationship management (CRM) services, with market leaders like SAP offering dozens of standardized product solutions as well as virtually unlimited custom solution development. However, in most of these cases the service provider is offering to perform and manage all three data-related activities, hosting storage and retrieval, pure data processing, and data analytics and reporting as well. So the label of *data processing* doesn't really apply, at least not in the way that it used to.

Separately, the consumer credit bureaus provide high-volume data processing services to institutions that use their scores in decision making and account management. While consumer banks are required to store their customer and transaction data in house, the credit bureaus themselves are providing a significant chunk of required data processing, but more importantly analytics, as the key component of their service offering.

For more critical data processing tasks like GL management and tax and other accounting applications, the trend has been to preserve internal physical control, especially for large firms. In these areas the big suppliers have shifted more towards the sale and maintenance of installable software platforms as well as support related consulting services. Other examples can be cited, but it seems evident that with the increasing importance of analytics and under the pressure to outsource storage and retrieval, this traditional external data processing marketplace has and may continue to shrink. At the same time, an even more pure form of external data processing is gaining importance as data volumes grow. This is the pure hosting of data processing in which the customer is responsible for all of the logic, control, and timing of the processing and the host passively provides computational capacity. Increasingly this has meant "cloud" computing, which means the processing is distributed over wide arrays of hardware with excess capacity. The hosts no longer need to have massive mainframes dedicated to third party processing, and they no longer need to provide programming support. This availability of accessible capacity can be an important part of an institutions strategic infrastructure design.

Analytics and Reporting

Analytics and reporting is the layer where virtually all of the information creation occurs, and hence, where an institution can create or fail to create most of its competitive advantage. It encompasses all of the modeling that a firm engages in. This layer is also the broadest and most fragmented set of activities of the three, and accordingly, the set of software products available in this space is similarly broad and fragmented. While it is generally true that each of these things require software purchased from outside vendors, two facts make this a fairly weak generalization. First, analytics and reporting is an area where an institution can meet certain specific needs with internally developed software should it so choose, and there are subspaces within modeling and analytics where internally developed software is almost a prerequisite. Secondly, there isn't always a clear distinction between vendor-provided software and internally developed software. In virtually every software application, the vendor brings something to the table and the users/analysts bring something to the table. The most obvious examples are spreadsheets. The spreadsheet application is vendor-supplied, but the valuable software is embedded in the spreadsheet by the user and so is internally developed. This pattern of blurring is repeated over most of the range of analytics and reporting software, from computer languages with embedded libraries of functions, to data mining and data visualization tools.

Importantly, the work performed under the umbrella of analytics and reporting consists of both known, regular, and often required processes and processes that are more ad hoc, entrepreneurial, and in many ways unpredictable. Reporting includes both the production of required financial disclosures and other regulatory requirements as well as discretionary disclosures and internal financial performance monitoring. Such processes tend to be quite stable over time, and are of course critical to the functioning of the firm. But a well-functioning firm, from this basic reporting requirements perspective, can still suffer loss of market share and degradation of performance over time.

More and more, it is the effectiveness of the analytic function that prevents these untoward outcomes by making sure that product and service design and pricing are competitive, that market intelligence is as rich and timely as possible, and that asset management can be performed at the highest level of effectiveness. All of these objectives depend on well resourced (where resourcing includes the availability of deep, wide-ranging, and high-quality data) analytics teams supplying timely information to decision makers.

However, because at the corporate level the finance organization is often viewed as the key constituent for the overall information processing infrastructure, firms often prioritize these basic reporting functions far above the analytic functions, at least from a resource allocation perspective. Two effects can result: (1) Effective current required reporting leads to an institutional complacency that the overall infrastructure is adequate so that required improvements for the analytic functions go unmet, and (2) an institutional resistance may develop toward the consideration of major infrastructure overhauls that do not improve (and may be viewed as potentially threatening to) these key reporting functions. System design changes that could support long-term improvements in analytics and hence improved profitability and competitiveness often take a back seat to comfort with current reporting capabilities. However, as we have discussed, reporting requirements continue to evolve in the direction of advanced analytics. CCAR is an example of a regulatory requirement that is on its surface a reporting requirement, but at its core is an exercise in advanced analytics. It has been a particularly frustrating exercise for firms whose analytics and reporting infrastructures have long been separated and maintained, planned for and resourced by different constituents. For those that can evolve their analytics and reporting functions as complementary components of a common integrated data model (discussed further in the section, "An Integrated Data Architecture"), the analytic quality of exercises like CCAR will inevitably go up and the cost of producing the final results (reports) will inevitably go down.

Strategic Resource Management

Because of the differences in the nature of the tasks that need to be accomplished by these three classes of tools, and because of the differences in the features, acquisition costs, and life cycles of the products themselves, it would seem appropriate to optimize the firms' resource spend separately for each stream. That is, firms should plan to meet their needs for storage and retrieval, data processing, and modeling and analytics separately, choosing products that give the highest bang for their buck within each process category. This allows the firm to opportunistically adopt new and improved technologies that become available in each of these three areas, without disturbing neighboring functions. A popular alternative approach is to embrace (at least over an identified range of activities) a software that performs all three functions in one integrated environment. SAS is certainly the leader in providing this kind of threefold capability under a single software umbrella, and many firms have extensive (so-called) SAS shops. But excellence at all three does not necessarily mean being the best at any one of them. The power of the traditional relational database/SQL technology for storage and retrieval is evidenced by its market dominance, and by the fact that even SAS contains an opt-out capability (PROC SQL), which allows the user to avoid using SAS data storage technology if desired. Advanced analytic modelers typically prefer more direct coding environments such as MATLAB, C++, S+, and R over the more indirect, precoded functionality of SAS. SAS's outstanding data processing capabilities make it the preferred product for super high-volume modeling applications like credit cards. But the question the resource planners need to ask is, how can we maximize the output of the analytic and reporting layer while expanding and maintaining the performance of the data storage and delivery function? In some cases, integrated multifunction products like SAS may be an important part of the solution.

Clearly, the deepest underlying core data system should be designed to support the long-range institutional goals for data acquisition and retention and for performance. When the institution has established future data volume goals, the system design can be optimized for performance at that capacity of storage and retrieval. As we will discuss later on, because institutions have a virtually unlimited ability to capture and purchase data from external sources, the volumes of data that they should be looking to store, process, and convert into information should be orders of magnitude higher than they have done historically. But beyond the motivating factor of potential external data acquisition, effective storage and accessibility of *internally generated* data also requires institutions to set much higher targets for the volume capability of their core system. The two reasons for this are that (1) effective and efficient system design requires that the core system be built on the most granular level possible, and (2) more historical data needs to be stored.

In most cases, this means that all transactional data and transactional data history, as well as detailed customer and client data and their histories, and high-frequency asset valuation and cash-flow data for investments, should be stored in the central core system. One practice that frustrates system integration is that of capturing and managing financial transaction data in account management systems that are upstream from the firm's GL system. In many cases, the GL is managed at a level of granularity/aggregation unto itself, wherein the vertical structuring of the data is likely to be aligned with the legal entity structure of the firm, and the horizontal aggregation may be at different levels of granularity, but not at the transactional level. The problem is aggravated when operating units manage subledgers at a level of granularity somewhere in between the account management systems and the corporate GL. In such cases, the need for and cost of reconciliations can be material. To support an efficient integration with risk systems that depend on transactional data (although a narrow range of data types), the central accounting system design must tie to transactional cash flows and transactional accounting adjustments—the so-called fat ledger approach. In this case, *tie to* is in fact a gross understatement. With an integrated and fully granular core system design, the GL is produced *directly from* the granular underlying data. Similarly, the risk data model consists of the same transactional and customer-level data. It may strike readers that expanding the volume of data flowing into the GL system to the individual cash-flow level is infeasible due to high data volumes; however, it should be borne in mind that what is being suggested relates to the system architecture only—*all of the granular data is already being stored*. It is the places that it is being stored and how it is stored that either facilitates or frustrates the integration of risk and finance systems.

As another example of where a lack of system integration can be a constraint, consider loss given default (LGD), a key risk data element. LGD exists in two forms: as an observed empirical quantity—*what did we lose?* (for defaulted credit exposures only)—and as an estimate for all existing credit exposures—*what would we expect to lose should the obligor default?* As we will discuss in Chapter 3 (along with the analogous PD), LGD estimation is an information-creating process and hence an opportunity for an institution to gain some marginal competitive advantage if it can compute LGD estimates better and faster than its peers. Many institutions have struggled with the calculation of empirical transactional LGD, particularly those who could benefit from it most: those who actively work out of default situations regularly, either because they expect to add value through this process or because their credit exposures are illiquid before or after default. That is, many lenders cannot easily and consistently answer the question, "How much did we lose?" on any given exposure to an obligor who defaulted. Naturally, the result is that their LGD models suffer from poor performance and have come under critical regulatory review since effective models to predict LGD cannot be produced without significant volumes of convincingly clean and consistent actual data. In part, a lack of good empirical LGD data can be traced to the fact that there is no natural constituency in whose interest it is to calculate and publish these statistics. But a lack of high quality LGD data can easily be seen as a more general data-processing gap. This is because each LGD observation is merely a discounted sum of cash flows—cash flows that must have been captured within some data repository. But in many cases, a default on a credit exposure will transfer the management of the account to a collections or workout department, whose operations and account management systems are unconnected with those used for performing credits. As a result, subsequent recovery cash flows may not be associated in any direct way with the exposure as originated. In some cases, a simple failure to preserve transaction identifiers as the control shifts from one department to another can cause this important information process to break down.

The inability to identify and direct underlying data toward satisfying the critical need of LGD calculation may be due to an ineffective data architecture, institutional ignorance, or both. Whether empirical transactional LGDs should be calculated and stored as part of a physical denormalization step or presented as calculations on the fly through a logical view is a question for the senior system architects to decide, but an obvious goal of the system design should be to present end users with real-time transactional LGD data, including not only completed transactional recoveries, but also current values for recoveries in progress. The inability to predict LGD is an information gap that can prevent underwriters from effectively adjusting terms, structure, and rates to reflect the underlying risk, as well as preventing traders from correctly assessing the inherent value of traded credit securities.

AN INTEGRATED DATA ARCHITECTURE

To accomplish the goal of very high volume efficiency and support the fully integrated model, the underlying core data structure needs to meet high performance standards for data retrieval and be appropriately scaled and highly normalized. Again, normalization simply means designing the database tables, their linkages, the form in which data are to be expressed for storage, and the indexing, coding, and dimensionality reduction that database architects apply to help the system store more and get it out faster. Typically, the science of such heavy levels of normalization is fully understood only by a handful of highly trained data architects who manage the needs of a particular institution. And while anyone with SQL experience *could* extract data from the normalized core, the structure is apt to be quite opaque without extensive training. Beyond those challenges for the individual user, there is high risk that inefficient queries, written by ill-informed query writers against the core structure, will impair the system response time and require DBA (database administration) attention to remediate. Therefore, a certain amount of denormalization needs to occur to protect the integrity and performance of the core system and to display a more user-friendly view of the data for users. As shown in Figure 2.1, denormalization should proceed in steps and should be targeted toward optimizing efficiency and ease of use in specific functional areas. For high-volume systems, initial steps away from the core model require physical replication of data in slightly denormalized structures targeting high levels of specialization, such as risk or finance. The choice of how many first-step physical denormalizations to support should be driven by the size and complexity of

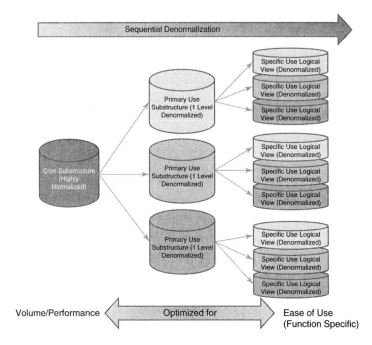

Figure 2.1 Stages of Denormalization for a Core Data Storage and Retrieval Model

the institution. It can be gauged from the degree of function-specific modeling that will be required in subsequent denormalization steps, as the data is brought ever closer to end users and information-creating processes and applications. Similarly, the choices about how to approach the logical view design—which and how many supported logical views to create and how to bridge into different parts of the analytic layer—will also be very institution-specific and may be driven by specific existing or desired features of the analytic layer.

Many other factors are also relevant in selecting the overall system design, and these design choices are among the most important choices an institution will make, as they will ultimately play a large role in determining the firm's competitive position with respect to information processing. Importantly, these choices *are* being made and must be made by every institution in operation. When they are made deliberately by informed senior leaders capable of establishing and communicating a vision, they are likely to be made well. When they are made by delegated managers responsible for only small pieces of the overall puzzle, or through neglect and a fear of separating from the legacy systems already in place, they are likely to be made poorly.

The factors that drive the choice between physical and logical denormalizations include those described next. Physical denormalizations (in which the data are physically transferred from a more normalized structure into a less normalized structure) are costly because they require bulk electronic transfer and load (ETL) capabilities at high frequency (lest the downstream data become stale), as well as additional hardware with consequent DBA support required. Physical denormalizations replicate data, which requires storage and consistency verification. Also, physical denormalizations are rigid, and any architectural design adjustment that may be needed at a later date will be very costly and time-consuming to effect. The cheaper and more flexible alternative is a logical denormalization, in which the data is simply reformatted and presented to the user as if the underlying data was resident in a simpler structure. Such logical views denormalize (simplify the appearance of) the data by eliminating unnecessary data elements and reconverting coded data into its natural form. The data is simply drawn from the true data structure *through* the logic that creates the view, so no data replication needs to occur. Logical views can even include additional data processing steps, from simple to highly complex that give the user more of what is actually needed than exists naturally in its more granular state in the underlying structure. Logical views, even with complex data processing embedded, can provide users with extremely low degradation in performance over what would be experienced by accessing the more normalized data structure directly. And of course, the goal of embedding such complex "logic" in the logical views is to greatly simplify the retrieval process for users, and the test of efficacy is that most of the required data extractions at each step should be accomplishable with simple SQL statements or other similar coded scripts.

Such a model is described generically in Figure 2.1. The design feature in which all of the data is stored in a core system on the left allows for a comprehensive data inventory to be maintained and for data ownership to be conclusively established and centrally managed—features that play an important role in both data quality management and in terms of system/process integration (topics discussed further in Chapters 4 and 7). As you move to the right in Figure 2.1, the data architecture becomes increasingly specialized and user-friendly, optimized for analytics and reporting, and intuitively designed to reduce training and errors. As you move to the left, the architecture is more optimized for fast retrieval, and ultimately on the far left, for both storage and retrieval at super high volume. This structure, composed of sequential reformatting of data from left to right, has one key design feature from which much of its benefit derives—as you move from left to right no new data from outside the system is added. It is this feature that eliminates reconciliation, and in so doing, can dramatically lower cost and reduce operational risk. In the integrated model, the data are prereconciled by virtue of how they are mapped, linked, and indexed within the core data structure.

An alternate design, which we'll call a disintegrated approach, involves the creation of many so-called data marts. These are physical data structures that may contain data pulled from anywhere inside or outside the firm. At many institutions, the proliferation of data marts has been so widespread that it is already a known controllership problem. Separately constructed and variously owned and administrated data marts create an opacity as to what data is where, where it came from, what its quality is, and who is using it for what. As an antithesis to an integrated information processing vision, it can be both a symptom and a cause. However, the devil is in the details. When data marts are constituted as specialized logical views utilizing the integrated core data model and acting to facilitate data access and use at the analytic layer (or slightly upstream from it), then these data marts are completely consistent with the integrated architecture approach. In fact, they are a critical part of the approach. When data marts make physical copies of existing data from disparate sources, or are the results of elementary data processing, then they are likely to be inconsistent with that vision unless they are sufficiently far upstream and designed to support multiple purposes. Highly specialized data marts of this kind should thus be viewed as red flags indicating a poorly communicated or executed vision. Finally, data marts that include data not already in the system (e.g., when they are initial entry points for internally generated or externally acquired data) are to be avoided. One obvious reason for this is that data not included in the underlying core data model may not be inventoried by those responsible for the overall architecture, and hence cannot be routed (or cannot be efficiently routed) to alternative users. Another is that such data marts are not under the purview of the system architects, and since data marts in general tend not to be highly normalized, data entering through them is unlikely to be normalized in accordance with overall design principles and hence will accumulate in an inefficient form. The avoidance of reconciliation requires that data be moving primarily outward from one common source toward reporting and analytics. Working from these principles, one can identify other red flags that indicate system design changes that are inconsistent with the principles and their objectives—a topic that we consider more carefully in Chapter 6.

Historically, multiple levels of physical denormalization were frowned upon as too costly, or a sign that the underlying architecture was poorly designed. When system architectures are designed for very specific functional uses, multiple physical instances of data may be difficult to defend. But these criticisms don't apply as well when the system design features a single originating database—a fully centralized model. In this case, the greater volume and breadth of data in the originating structure may make additional smaller and less normalized physical instances of data efficient from an ease-of-use perspective.

Another reason that this approach to system architecture doesn't get traction is that invariably there is no single underlying data model on the far left to denormalize, and firms see their immediate problem as cross-integrating multiple, currently disintegrated source systems. A classic example is when risk and finance (and often HR and marketing) have developed fully independent architectures. In such cases, a step-one denormalization may be unnecessary because the two systems are highly specialized already. But of course, the diagram in Figure 2.1 doesn't define what a single database is, and the traditional canister symbol belies the fact that each database contains an unlimited number of tables, queries, and other objects. The existence of two source databases suggests the absence of any common linkages that, were they to exist, would enable us to call the conglomerate structure a single database. Using data from two systems at the same time, as might be required (for example) to produce CCAR results, is difficult if the systems do not have any common identifying data fields or otherwise forged links, (i.e. are not integrated) or if their base granularity or other deep architectural features are incompatible.

The Data Hub Approach

When separate systems have evolved over time with no common linkages or common structural features, they can be almost impossible to fully integrate after the fact. Nevertheless, the effort to tie together independently developed and managed systems currently constitutes a hotbed of activity in the industry. In particular, enterprise-level platform vendors are now hawking preconsolidation platforms wherein the institution builds a new integrated source system and feeds it from disparate upstream source systems, creating a design often known as a risk-finance "data hub", since integrating risk and finance systems is usually the largest and most pressing problem (see Figure 2.2). Trying to solve system disintegration problems with the hub strategy can be problematic. Obviously, the continued existence of multiple core source systems preserves the need and cost for reconciliations of various kinds, and even if those reconciliations are considered part of the hub it is not clear how the cost is lowered or the efficiency improved through the creation of the intermediate warehouse. As observed by the FSA,

> Many firms had invested in or are planning to invest in a centralized "data warehouse" as a way of addressing the various data-management requirements of Solvency II. However, data warehouses are not a solution to the problem of combining data from disparate source systems, unless the data can be used in the destination systems in a meaningful way.[3]

The hub approach also typically involves a physical replication and storage of large amounts of data. From an overall performance and maintenance perspective, such bulk replication is to be avoided. As discussed above, we acknowledge that physical replication can be an important part of the system design, increasing efficiency when

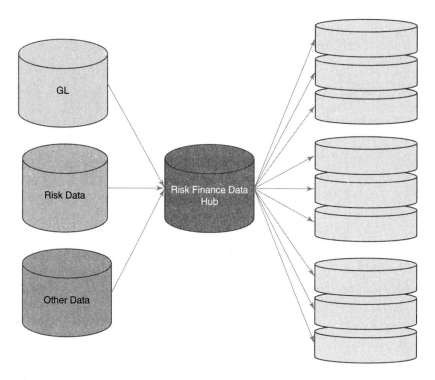

Figure 2.2 Multisourced Hub Style Data Model

it represents a step in a targeted denormalization scheme, especially when the core system contains very high volumes of highly normalized data. Renormalization of data that requires reconciliation is not likely to be serving the same purpose. Worse still are schemes in which the data from upstream sources are not integrated meaningfully in the hub, but co-located, with integration and reconciliation still to be performed. What has been accomplished in such cases is merely that data has been moved to the same (brand of) platform—a tiny benefit for the firm, but a big win for the vendor.

As an interim step toward a centralized model, the hub approach may be an expedient (and possibly the only practical) first step in a multigenerational plan. However, as a longer-term design it has structural suboptimalities even if the reconciliation and integration problems have been solved. Recalling the integrated model presented in Figure 2.1, the responsiveness of the system to changing demands is tied to its sequential nature, with a stable but flexible core data structure feeding increasingly flexible downstream structures. The hub introduces a rigidity in the middle of the process that will produce institutional and cost constraints to critical evolutionary change. That is, with upstream and downstream system characteristics driven by the structure of the hub, change on either side necessitates a change in the hub itself, which will likely have secondary ripple effects both up- and downstream. Significantly modifying the risk data system, for example, would entail a significant redesign of the hub, which would in turn require the redesign of downstream data structures and components of the analytic layer. The additional rigidity introduced by a hub approach comes with no real gain, since the integration of upstream systems (to the extent that it is desired or required) could have been accomplished directly across the upstream systems without ever creating a hub.

When the hub approach is used without full integration, it can also create problems of embedded data redundancy. By embedded data redundancy, we mean either situations in which data is processed into synonymous or analogous quantities and stored separately for different uses, or those in which like data elements are stored in different systems without enough identifying information to reconcile them automatically. Often data created through aggregation and other reporting processes end up being treated as core data as opposed to processed results. This, and a lack of coherent data ownership and control, can lead to similar but not equivalent definitions being used simultaneously, creating confusion and unnecessary additional reconciliation requirements. For example, suppose a business unit totals up sales within an account management system based on a 30-day month and physically stores that amount in a local data mart. Suppose further that data from the business unit feeds a corporate GL system with an ETL script that uses calendar time, where the data is also stored. In this case, there appears to be two sources of the same data that will not be identical and will require a reconciliation. Without identifying this issue in advance and addressing it with an upstream integration, both values may end up in the hub with identical or slightly different field names. Contrast that with a model in which granular sales information is stored in a single repository and all downstream users need to access the data by query. In this case, alternate monthly sales data can be created on the fly from the same source tables, does not need to be stored physically, and never requires reconciliation.

But the problems described above apply to the hub approach even in the ideal case in which all downstream processes and uses of data emanate from the hub. In practice, institutions often employ the hub approach for a narrow set of purposes, or even a single purpose, such as CCAR. In cases such as these, many processes continue to exist in which the data flow is directly downstream from the multiple originating source systems *in addition to the hub-based processes*. In such cases, data redundancies are almost certainly going to increase, and data quality control efforts (as discussed further in Chapter 6), located to support the hub, will not fully span the controlled data elements being used directly from the source systems. Moreover, while the hub can house some centralized reconciliation processes, the continued flow of like data from source systems that *do not* pass through the hub mean these reconciliations will be incomplete and may need to be repeated elsewhere or simply not performed to support all uses. In summary, a hub approach that is not comprehensive (i.e., when the hub is serving the role of a fully integrated centralized source system) will

- Add complexity.
- Add rigidity to the overall system.
- Frustrate the efficient deployment of data quality controls.
- Increase the likelihood that costly data reconciliation efforts are incomplete.

Organizing System Components

How should the three process components fit together physically? Taking the basic storage and retrieval structure from Figure 2.1, we can layer on the other two types of critical software we identified in the previous section: data processing and analytics and reporting. As shown in Figure 2.3, it is evident that the one of the goals of successive denormalization is to replace or reduce the need for data processing proper. Therefore, the institution can design its core architecture first, allow

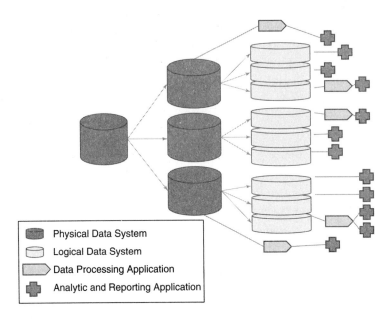

Figure 2.3 Sequential Structuring of Data Processing Components

the analytics and reporting tools to be highly fragmented and driven by user demands, and bridge the gaps, where needed, with targeted data processing components. That is, dedicated data processing can be used as a cheaper alternative to additional denormalization when needs are very highly specialized or relatively transient, or when it is convenient to preserve some features of a more normalized data structure. This configuration is presented in Figure 2.3, which simply adds the additional software components to Figure 2.1 in an illustrative way. In Figure 2.3 the crosses represent models, analytic tools used for modeling, reporting applications, and analytical tools used for reporting. As we discuss further in this chapter, these are the means by which data elements are converted into information. Therefore, maximizing the quality and volume-based productivity of the analytic and reporting layer should be the ultimate goal of the storage and retrieval and data processing layers.

Again, this basic architecture is designed to exploit and enable the dynamics of the component parts that include the data itself and the changing business uses. On the left-hand side, the pure storage and retrieval elements are based on the slowest moving technology—the physical storage, physical data structural elements, and SQL language that have remained in place since the mid-1970s and are supported by every major vendor. Logical data structures (in the center of the diagram) are also based on this same stable technology, but their designs are completely under the institution's control and may evolve at different rates depending on what the institution needs to respond to. Pure data processing components can be applied using a variety of specific software applications, which can be swapped out as needed to take advantage of ongoing technological advances in this space. Finally, the design is supportive of, and agnostic to, the individual components in the analytic layer, which, as we have described, consists of a froth of highly fragmented, specialized, and rapidly changing applications. To make this more concrete we might include in such a list vendor-provided analytic tools (such as SAS, MATLAB, R/S+, C++/C#, Java, Python, Stata, and Eviews) as well as reporting tools (such as Excel, Business Objects, Spotfire, and many, many more). Of course, to these would need to be added all of the proprietary analytic and reporting tools an institution might develop.

As a final point on this topic, note that an institution with a centralized data model will need a system for granting and maintaining data access rights. It is likely that demands for access to specific data will be as complex and dynamic as the analytic activities themselves. The sequential structuring scheme identifies the appropriate place for the administration of data access rights—the interface between the logical data model administrators and the analysts requesting the data. In fact, this is basically what the logical data modelers are doing anyway when they are designing their data views. This also creates an optimal balance of understanding of the need/request and ability to respond. Lastly, it insulates the core system engineers from requests that require them to investigate and protects the core data delivery structures from any performance degradation that could result from permissions systems that are further upstream.

In fact, Figure 2.3 is missing an important component, although adding it to the diagram or actually building it out would not be particularly difficult. The missing part is the loop back from the analytic layer to the physical data storage system. This is critical, since the bulk of model outputs and other created information requires storage for later use and for process monitoring and measurement. What is important is to distinguish between elemental data stored in the deepest underlying core model, from which the entire information flow emanates, and the outputs of the process created within the analytic layer. It is also important to note that, for the purposes of monitoring the output and performance of the analytic layer (discussed further is Chapter 5), this output data needs to be stored in a data model that reflects the composition of the analytic layer and allows each data element to maintain enough identifying information (metadata) to associate it with a specific process and date. Because this data model needs to reflect the detailed characteristics of the analytic layer (and as we have discussed, the analytic layer is apt to be highly dynamic), a particularly flexible and specialized data model will likely be required. For this reason, if we did add this missing component to Figure 2.3 we would probably not direct arrows from the crosses back to the core physical data repository, but would direct them to a separate physical data system. We discuss this further in Chapter 6, and Figure 4.5 provides an illustration.

INFORMATION PROCESSING EFFICIENCY AS AN INSTITUTIONAL OBJECTIVE

A strategic vision for an enterprise data processing architecture, and for acquiring and maintaining hardware and software aligned with that vision, is a critical component in developing a competitively advantaged financial institution. We've focused on one aspect of the strategic design objective: the ability to store, retrieve, and process data in volumes far higher than have been targeted historically, in support of a diverse and dynamic analytic and reporting layer capable of producing more information from that higher volume of stored data. We should not lose sight of a critical and closely related strategic objective—effective controllership and quality assurance for the data itself, data processing, and analytics and reporting.

System Design Considerations

Such a vision is not easy to implement, nor will it pay off as expected unless it is nested within an organizational operating model with roles, responsibilities, and specific personnel choices made to align with and support that information processing model. In particular, a commitment to a vastly more capable and vastly more efficient information processing model must include a commitment to create a human capital model that can support that commitment. It is important to do away with, or at least meaningfully remediate, the IT rift discussed in Chapter 1. To accomplish this, it will be necessary to elevate the importance of the information processing layer—the crosses in Figure 2.3. As we discuss in more detail in Chapter 3, it is this layer that converts data elements into information, and the speed, volume, and tactical targeting of information creation is what will ultimately determine the competitive position of the institution. When the servicing of the information conversion layer is prioritized as the objective, there is a teleology established for all of the upstream activities, including data capture and storage, and each subsequent step of data processing. This includes not only the physical IT infrastructure, but also the organizational structure and the roles and responsibilities of teams supporting specific components of the overall model. Each activity must be a deliberate piece of teamwork.

It might seem tempting, and in many respects intuitive, to try to work backward from the analytic layer in stages, to see that each stage appropriately supports the next, with the core storage architecture design being the final result of this induction, dictated by the needs of the first set of normalized structures. In practice, however, this is not a productive approach. There are two reasons to design the system from the bottom up, working from the core storage system outward toward the analytic layer. First, the analytic layer is, and should be, highly dynamic. The problems being solved through the information creation process are ever changing, and the tools used to produce models and analyses are also rapidly evolving and shifting with the flow of personnel and their preferences and experience. In one period critical marketing analyses may be produced by a particular team predominately using MATLAB. In a subsequent period, a completely different problem in asset liability management (ALM) may be being worked on in MATLAB as well, possibly allowing for the transfer of highly skilled analysts (along with their software) from the marketing department to compliance. Other shops may depend critically on SAS but then may suddenly need to adopt alternative tools for specific problems. The environment is similar for reporting: Tools continue to evolve technologically, with new data visualization tools like Spotfire increasing the power and speed of data analysis. As described in Figure 2.3, the goal of the complete data processing system design is to support a frenetic churn of analyses and modeling using an equally frenetic churn of software applications adopted to perform each task. This is accomplished by staging in a number of layers of fixed denormalization to specialize the data structure for certain classes of activity, followed by a number of layers (primarily logical) of denormalization intended to create both additional specialization along with flexibility. Finally, the system is augmented with dedicated pure data processing components designed to enhance that flexibility at the point where the analytic layer begins.

As the foregoing discussion was intended to highlight, effective system design involves answering these key questions:

● How many nodes of physical denormalization should we support?

● At which points should we transition from physical data models to logical data models?

● At which points do we bridge between layers with applied data processing software?

Answering these questions, along with "How much data should we plan to store?" is at the core of developing a strategy for data storage and retrieval, which is itself the foundation of a strategy for information processing. As we will discuss further in Chapter 3, given that we are living increasingly in a Big Data world and that competitive advantages will accrue to those who can efficiently capture and process larger and larger amounts of the right data, financial institutions need to be on the leading edge of developing and tuning high-volume information processing architectures. As discussed earlier, hardware, software, and personnel investments and allocations need to be aligned with some common vision. This cannot occur unless the institution has such a vision, ensures that the vision has been well articulated and is fully supported by senior leadership, and commits to communicating the vision openly through all layers and functions. Each layer and function has to understand what it needs to do to align with and support the vision, and what benefits beyond overall firm competitiveness it is likely to get from it. In particular, if the firm is to establish support of the analytic layer as a high-priority goal, it will need also to establish metrics against this goal that it can use to measure individual and group performance. We consider some function-specific performance metrics next.

The Human Capital Component

The vision for deploying human capital needs to be aligned with the overall system design, but more importantly, it needs to be aligned with the very concept of a firm-wide vision for information processing. That is, a broader form of teamwork is required within the firm—broader than what is typically found in financial institutions today. At each point in the data management/information processing flow, individuals need to be placed to help make that specific step more efficient and effective and to protect the integrity of the overall vision. To do this, each such individual must have expertise in and an understanding of the neighboring steps in the relevant process, as well as an understanding of where the step in question fits into the overall process design. This is another reason why the data should flow in one direction from the core storage system through multiple stages of denormalization and/or data processing and finally into the analytic layer.

Ultimately, the requirements for the types of information creation that can produce some competitive advantage lie in the expertise and creative vision of the actuaries, statisticians, econometricians, and other analysts who recognize where decision making can be improved and understand how to improve it. It is the entrepreneurial power of this analytic work that is responsible for expanding the information-creating potential of the firm. Because of this, this analytic community needs to be empowered to establish the priorities for data acquisition and delivery and to determine the software and other tools needed to maximize the efficiency of their individual functions. With those priorities established, the rest of the information processing teams can establish their own priorities and timelines to achieve the evolving objectives. The unidirectional sequencing of the data flow makes the purpose of each step, and how that step

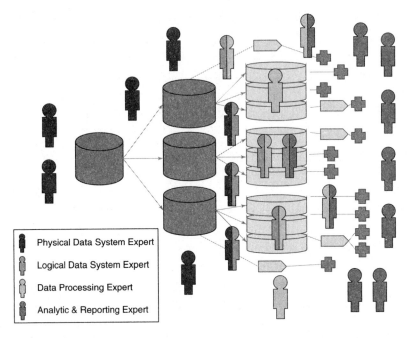

Figure 2.4 Alignment of Personnel with the Specific Data Processing Structure

serves to meet the objectives set by the analytic teams, more clear to all of the participants, defining (or at least clarifying) the roles and responsibilities of individuals supporting specific system and/or process components.

As shown in Figure 2.4, the specific skills required combine business subject matter expertise with expertise in the data processes a few steps upstream and a few steps downstream from the immediate data processing activity. For this architecture to function effectively, it needs to evolve efficiently, and efficient evolution requires system managers at each layer of data promotion and distribution who can receive and respond to downstream requests for system enhancements and new data sources. For example, managing the core data storage structure is a discipline that needs to focus on data acquisition and on the science of high-volume database efficiency. Because the job of staging data for use (any use, but especially indirect use) is delegated to the managers of downstream data structures, upstream managers can focus myopically on efficiency—defined as high-volume retrieval performance. These skills need to be recognized and demanded of the personnel tasked with performing this function, and their job performance ratings must be explicitly tied to excellence in these specific areas. Similarly, the second stage—wherein smaller, more specialized, derivative physical databases are built and maintained—also requires a specific set of skills. These again include high-volume efficient database design and the experience to work in a highly controlled production environment. But these system managers need more expertise in designing and managing the ETL processes by which these downstream databases get refreshed than their upstream counterparts. They will also have constituents: the working groups for whom these more specialized data structures are designed. Since these data structures will still be highly normalized and specialized only in certain high-level respects, relevant business constituents are apt to be quite senior, with wide-ranging responsibilities. As such, the right kind of communication skills and a service-minded approach will be critical to the success of these system managers, and (again) these skills will need to be deliberately targeted in hiring and used to evaluate performance.

At the next set of data promotion points, data technicians create and maintain logical data views as opposed to physical data models. This allows them to be continually tailored and adjusted to meet user demands without requiring any change in the upstream physical structures. Naturally, a separate set of technical skills is required to write the transformation routines and create the logical objects that will trade off the benefits of specialization with the requirements of performance. But also, as Figure 2.4 shows, multiple logical data views are likely to be created from each stage-two physical model—perhaps many dozens, or more. Hence, these data technicians will need to be more specialized and far more numerous. They will also need to work more closely, in a service-provider capacity, with users who are far closer to the downstream analytic work. Key performance metrics, such as response times and customer satisfaction measures, will be more service oriented. Again, the selection and evaluation for technicians installed in this layer need to be appropriately specialized. We have belabored the point somewhat, but at the risk of repetition, it may be worth reemphasizing that these recommendations about staffing cannot be implemented without an HR organization that itself has deep domain expertise in these specific areas and is itself fully cognizant of the overall vision.

A DIGRESSION ON UNSTRUCTURED DATA

Recent changes in thinking and in analytic capability have expanded the definition of data significantly, increasing the supply of data by several orders of magnitude in the process. The days in which data consisted of easy-to-store and easy-to-process binary representations of numerical quantities are gone. In particular, all text is now considered data, and even this incalculably large expansion is nested within a broader category known as *unstructured data* that includes multimedia objects as well as blended media objects. *Computerworld* states that unstructured data might account for more than 70 to 80 percent of all data in organizations—a conservative estimate given that every word in every document ever produced is now considered data. Advances in computer analytics include techniques designed to analyze and mine unstructured data of various kinds, including new storage and retrieval technologies (such as MongoDB,[4] an open-source storage technology) and new techniques, such as sharding and hashing, for applying structure and structured querying to more unstructured data types. These techniques themselves, while fascinating, can be somewhat esoteric compared to the routine data management and information processing requirements of financial institutions. As a body of work, these new techniques are opening up new potential in social science research. In particular, social sentiment monitoring techniques are already showing great promise in modeling customer behavior for marketing purposes, and in monitoring broader social trends that help measure political risk. However, while complex data mining algorithms designed to be applied to unlimited digitized text such as those described in "A Time-Efficient Breadth-First Level-Wise Lattice-Traversal Algorithm to Discover Rare Itemsets"[5] do show promise, these algorithms provide little to help financial institutions trying to price products and services, raise capital, and comply with the wide variety of regulatory reporting requirements that ensure their survival.

However, some industry analysts are suggesting that institutions radically rethink their strategies for data processing and information management in terms of this new definition and these new techniques. The idea being advanced is that since unstructured data swamps structured data by volume, firms should stop focusing on designing efficient data structures and focus on better designs for processing unstructured data. Certainly, there is much to be learned from these pioneering efforts that could ultimately prove transformative. And from the perspective of competitive advantage, the ability to outpace peers in the creation of usable information from unstructured data may ultimately be decisive. Nevertheless, the current dialogue in the industry includes an alarming and extreme line of discussion about which current technologies are *constraints* on efficiency. As we have argued, one of the critical enablers of effective information processing is the effective design of key data storage and retrieval systems. That is, intelligent structuring of data is of the *highest* priority in terms of its effect on efficient information processing and ultimately on competitiveness. It is probably safe to say (competitive advantages at the margin notwithstanding) that better than 99 percent of the data that a financial institution needs to access on a routine basis is, and will continue to be, of the structured variety—and as highly structured as possible. Under the alternate view, the technology of structuring data can be seen as secondary to the technology of processing unstructured data. This is hard to accept given that there is no academic or industry consensus on what constitutes a data model for unstructured data, or whether such a thing could ever exist. Consider the following statement from a major data processing vendor:

> Companies that can manage the volume and variety of data in an agile manner can react better to shifting consumer preferences and changing market conditions, which means ongoing business advantage. One practice that stands in the way is based on a technical anachronism that views structured data and unstructured content as two separate worlds.

Treating structured and unstructured data as comparable phenomena that ought to be treated within the same paradigm means denigrating the value of data structure, that is, the importance of the data system architecture. This upside down thinking can be packaged as good news for institutions unwilling or unable to address systemic deficiencies in how they structure their key data repositories. In some cases institutions are being told by software vendors, "Don't worry about redesigning your core data storage capabilities to organize key data in an efficient centralized data repository—we can address the fact that your data is poorly structured with unstructured data techniques."

NOTES

1. Unstructured data is discussed in more detail later in this chapter in the section "A Digression on Unstructured Data."

2. See, for example, the so-called CAP theorem attributed to Eric Brewer, introduced at the Symposium on Principles of Distributed Computing 2000 Symposium on Principles of Distributed Computing, Berkley The CAP (consistency, availability, partition tolerance) theorem summarizes trade-offs inherent in decades of distributed-system designs, and shows that maintaining a single-system image in a distributed system has a cost.

3. Financial Services Authority, "Solvency II: Internal Model Approval Process Thematic Review Findings," February 2011, 8. www.macs.hw.ac.uk/~andrewc/erm2/reading/FSA.InternalModelApprovalProcess.pdf.

4. www.mongodb.org.

5. Luigi Troiano and Giacomo Scibelli, "A Time-Efficient Breadth-First Level-Wise Lattice-Traversal Algorithm to Discover Rare Itemsets," *Data Mining and Knowledge Discovery* 28, no. 3 (May 2014): 773–807.

CHAPTER **3**

Data, Models, and Information

I n this chapter, we define models and their role in information processing and in generating competitive advantage for financial institutions. We discuss model risk, and the model governance boom that began in the years before the 2008 crisis and intensified as a result of the crisis, largely under pressure from systemic regulators like the Fed. We explain why firms looking to develop long-term competitive advantages will likely view existing regulatory requirements as bare minima that can easily be met when information processing capabilities are appropriately prioritized.

MODEL RISK MANIA

Beginning in the late 1990s and taking an enormous leap following the 2008 financial crisis, the financial services industry has been beset with demands for greater recognition of model risk, better capabilities for measuring it, and comprehensive and effective model governance. These demands have come from investors, regulators, managers, commentators, and the general public. The clear implication is that bad decisions and general mismanagement leading to huge losses and institutional collapse can be traced to a lack of quality control in the analytic layer. The fact that financial institutions had long been evolving toward a more quantitative, information-processing model was known to many observers, including bank regulators who stated in the introduction of their main model risk guidance memo that

> Banks rely heavily on quantitative analysis and models in most aspects of financial decision making. They routinely use models for a broad range of activities, including underwriting credits; valuing exposures, instruments, and positions; measuring risk; managing and safeguarding client assets; determining capital and reserve adequacy; and many other activities. In recent years, banks have applied models to more complex products and with more ambitious scope, such as enterprise-wide risk measurement, while the markets in which they are used have also broadened and changed. Changes in regulation have spurred some of the recent developments, particularly the U.S. regulatory capital rules for market, credit, and operational risk based on the framework developed by the Basel Committee on Banking Supervision. Even apart from these regulatory considerations, however, banks have been increasing the use of data-driven, quantitative decision-making tools for a number of years.[1]

But while the recognition of the growing importance of quantitative methods in a wider range of financial institution activities may have been growing since the 1970s, it seemed to linger behind the scenes in the minds of market participants until the mid-1990s. Up until that time, the Federal Reserve Bank of New York did not have the formal Models and Methodologies Department that it has today, nor did it have the formal model governance exams that it regularly conducts today. Examinations of analytic and model-related risks were conducted through the Risk Assessment Unit within the Bank Supervision Division. Obviously, there was no SIFI[2] status, so no nonbank entities were in scope. An important transition in perspective within the Fed came in 1994 during an examination of Banker's Trust. At that time, Banker's Trust was an institution in the process of shifting its focus from traditional commercial banking toward derivatives trading and brokering, specifically in the relatively noncommoditized areas of bespoke rate and foreign exchange (FX) derivatives. During that exam the Risk Assessment Unit learned of the existence of a wide array of proprietary models used to price and structure these innovative products. The unit then recognized that the performance and even the solvency of the institution could hinge on the effectiveness and control of these models. The Fed came to understand that it could not evaluate the health of such an institution without evaluating the strength of its technical modeling, and a fledgling model risk assessment function was born.

Model-Based Financial Products Boom

A survey of the industry developments that paralleled the evolving regulatory perspective helps to provide context for the current state of affairs. It's worth noting that the importance of models in the financial services industry is as old as the industry itself and that the importance of programmed statistical models precedes the development of flexible computer data systems, networks, and even PCs. An antecedent to the popular bond pricing models now provided by firms like Algorithmics can be found in the bond pricing algorithms of Monroe built into self-contained desktop calculators and sold from the mid-1970s up through the late 1980s. Figure 3.1 below is a photo of (my own)

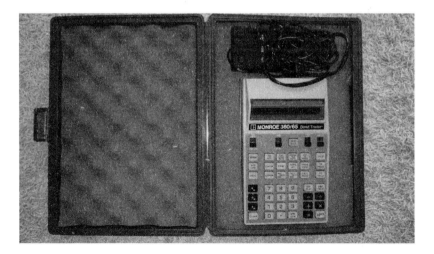

Figure 3.1 A Classic Model: The Monroe 360

Monroe 360 calculator circa 1978, which was something of an industry standard and may still be in use today. Certainly model-based mutual funds had been growing in success and number since the mid-1970s as well. But the emergence of clearly systemic types of model risk might be traced to the mid-1990s when collateralized bond obligations (CBOs) were emerging as a hot investment product.

These CBOs represented a great strategic complement to the boom in speculative-grade bond issuance that had begun in the early 1990s. For financial institutions, the fee income generated by creating high-dollar denominated investment products with high credit ratings and superior yields was proving to be material. The "models" behind this investment boom were primarily the CBO models used by the two major ratings agencies to rate and structure CBO tranches. Easily reverse-engineered by banks to do prospective analysis, these models contained strong but weakly supported assumptions about correlations in credit movement, largely based on historical ratings transitions patterns, and assumptions about default rates that underplayed the "through-the-cycle" characteristic of their own ratings. Essentially, deal managers could bundle up a bunch of BBB-rated bonds, tranche them, and produce a whopping AAA-rated tranche which could be sold off for a few bps of premium and capture the underlying yield differential. However, the validity of the models underlying the ratings on these tranches had not been established. Without sufficiently robust analytics, deep historical supporting data, and some theory about which features of the historical patterns in the data were likely to remain stable and which were likely to change the quality of the tranche, ratings were inevitably poor. In fact, these ratings would not even have qualified as information as per the definition advanced in this chapter, since the probabilistic loss characteristics of the tranches were effectively unknown.

To many observers, the agency CBO models were creating a rating-grade arbitrage opportunity, since the favorable conversion rate from lower grades to AAA through pooling and tranching was being managed by the agencies themselves, using models that had not been sufficiently or independently validated and that had the appearance of bias. The core questions that needed to be answered to infuse the tranche ratings with information were (1) what is the term structure of default risk associated with each of the names in a given pool, (2) how independent/how correlated are those default probabilities over time, and (3) what are the likely loss/recovery values associated with sets of correlated default realizations at various levels of likelihood for the latter? Yet the information used to answer these questions consisted largely of historical averages (or smooth functions of historical averages) of data compiled by the main rating agencies. Few alternate data sources and limited independent analyses were brought to bear.

The asset class evolved as fixed-pool CBOs gave way to managed CBOs, in which managers could trade bonds in and out of the structure within fixed structural limits, potentially boosting the performance and extending the life of the structure while adding additional uncertainty from a statistical perspective as to how to characterize the loss probabilities on the derivative exposures. An important transition occurred when banks began viewing this technology and the related investment trend as a potential funding source. The largest banks began using synthetic collateralized debt obligations (CDOs) to move exposure off-balance sheet, taking advantage of attractive funding rates and freeing up capital. All of this seemed like banking at its best—efficient pooling of risk, and both intermediation as the syndicated loan market was stimulated and disintermediation as the risk pools were put back into the capital markets. The market for CDOs tied to mortgages and mortgage-backed securities (discussed in more detail in Chapter 6) had also begun to grow exponentially. But on the basis of what information were these poolings and redistributions of risk taking place? At the time, there seemed to be a presumption that *these transactions could not be taking place unless supported by adequate information flows to all critical participants.* However, as a variety of high-profile defaults and the collapse of the mortgage-backed CDO market were to reveal, this presumption was not well founded.

While model-based investment products were becoming more and more systemically important, model-based consumer financial products were also exploding. To a large extent, this was manifest not in the introduction of wholly new products, but in the greater use of sophisticated models to greatly expand existing products like credit cards, consumer loans, auto loans, and mortgages. The features of these products evolved more and more to reflect perceived behavioral tendencies and risk characteristics, and aggregate exposures expanded dramatically as a result. Securitization, using the same basic technologies described above, helped fund the boom in consumer credit products and push them into riskier and riskier products and subsegments of the population.

Although prior to 2008 many regulators and policy commentators thought that poor model governance practices at financial institutions represented significant idiosyncratic and systemic risk, after the crisis of 2008 this view broadened significantly. The way regulators thought about systemic risk mitigation began to evolve as well. Before the crisis the prevailing view was that regulators could establish capital adequacy and liquidity rules through what was effectively an academic process and then, knowing what to do, simply establish sufficiently conservative capital rules. Once the rules were established, they could use their examination processes to compel institutions to conform to them. But as the crisis began to unfold, regulators came to perceive more clearly that they themselves were dependent on the information flow produced by the many individual institutions to monitor the current health and potential changes in trend within the system as a whole. Now better information processing was not simply a standard to be imposed on institutions to insure they protected themselves with financial system stability being an indirect byproduct. Now it was the lynchpin of a new type of regulatory regime in which the regulators would demand the information for themselves, to actively manage systemic stability. Under this new view, a fully informed regulator could see systemic risks coming well in advance and could take steps to thwart them. As long as sufficient information was flowing, protecting the health of at-risk individual institutions was no longer paramount, no longer particularly relevant, and perhaps not even desirable. As early as 2009 the FSB (Financial Stability Board) prepared a report entitled "The Financial Crisis and Information Gaps" espousing this theory, stating

> While the financial crisis was not the result of a lack of
> proper economic and financial statistics, it exposed a
> significant lack of information as well as data gaps on key
> financial sector vulnerabilities relevant for financial

stability analysis. Some of these gaps affected the dynamics of the crisis, as markets and policy makers were caught unprepared by events in areas poorly covered by existing information sources, such as those arising from exposures taken through complex instruments and off-balance sheet entities, and from the cross-border linkages of financial institutions.[3]

This shift of focus from rule following to the more comprehensive creation and dissemination of information is discussed in more detail later in this chapter in the "Regulatory Regimes and Guidance" section.

The Model Governance Industry Wakes Up

As a boon to a particular set of stakeholders, the recent model governance boom has created a demand for consulting firms that is almost without precedent. Demand for advice with respect to interpreting regulatory requirements, policy drafting, and the structuring and management of model validation teams, as well as demand for direct model validation services, have kept the big consulting firms very busy for the past five to 10 years and caused many others to spring up. This tremendous demand for external resources highlights the degree to which financial institutions have struggled and continue to struggle with this particular function. Conferences on model governance now occur monthly, if not weekly, and these conferences function almost like sporting industry events in which players mill about shopping for teams while team leaders mill about shopping for players. Salaries for experienced model validators have skyrocketed, while the retention rates at major financial institutions and at regulatory agencies have trended down. Software vendors have rushed into the market with products that range from model validation toolkits and model inventory applications to full model governance systems designed for large institutions and offered as add-ons to comprehensive data and application systems.

Attraction and retention issues aside, organizational challenges similar to those that exist in the IT realm also frequently exist in the model governance/model risk management space. Few senior leaders spent significant amounts of their careers doing model governance or model risk management work, so the alliances between these functional leaders and senior management have tended to be weak. More tactically, senior leaders are usually unable to get a meaningful summary (inventory) of what their analytic assets are, and what the risk/return characteristics of those assets look like. Model validation teams are perceived as adding value only when a model fails or the teams are otherwise critical of a model, which invariably makes some business leader unhappy. Model governance is then simply a costly compliance function at best, and possibly a nuisance, as opposed to a function that serves to improve the quality of the flow of critical information throughout the firm. Part of this is due, to the lack of a framework for assessing analytic and data assets on a risk/reward basis, which will be discussed in Chapter 6. Part of it has to do with the level of understanding embedded in the upper layers of the management chain. While banks and other financial institutions have been willing to hire experienced quants (quantitative analysts) to lead model validation teams, they are often more structurally isolated than people leading other comparable functions. Some firms have structured themselves to have the model validation function roll up under operational risk, while others have it roll up under internal audit; for those that have it roll up under risk, there is often a reporting layer between that function and the chief risk officer (CRO), an arrangement that can effectively create a barrier to communication and information transfer.

As discussed in Chapter 1, when this middle-reporting layer involves a general manager without deep domain expertise in modeling, it can be concluded that the barrier is intentional, installed because the value placed on the potential information flow is low. Worse still are the so-called "decentralized" models in which management of model validation and model governance are left to the individual business units. Under this arrangement senior managers cannot obtain consolidated reporting on anything beyond basic policy compliance, and under these conditions meaningful quantitative understanding of model risk at the firm level and the risk/return characteristics of individual models are infeasible. As usual, this stems from the institution not viewing the management of its analytic assets as a core competency at which it must excel to compete, but rather as largely a compliance exercise. Certainly, there is a higher likelihood that an institution will view model risk management this way if it also views IT as merely a supporting function that can be evaluated only on a costs basis. We discuss the model governance process in more detail in Chapter 4.

DEFINITIONS AND EPISTEMOLOGY

Without question, the world's consumption and use of data and information has burgeoned over the past few decades. The methods for generating data have multiplied and the cost of data storage has dropped to the point where data accumulation seems to have outpaced the needs of the human species. Digital images alone are accumulating at a rate that would preclude viewing them all subsequently, and numerical data of every type is being pumped into an ever-expanding array of proprietary and cloud-based storage media at a rate that can only be guessed at. And one of the amazing and stark facts about this growth is that the flow of data far exceeds what data users can capture and use at a later date. For example, a University of San Diego study[4] found that Americans used 3.6 zettabytes of total data in their homes in 2008. Even though that astronomical number excludes all business users, it is roughly 20 times more than what could be stored on all the hard drives in the world at that time. In other words, because communication of every kind is increasingly digital, and even with all of the increase in data storage capacity currently deployed, *the flow of data generated by human activity swamps our capacity to store it*. Therefore, the ability to identify, filter out, and store high value-in-use data is a critical component of developing a competitive advantage in information. As we suggested in Chapter 2, the amount of data a financial institution (even a very selective and specialized one) should attempt to capture and store for later processing should be determined through some structured analytic process and should probably be orders of magnitude higher than would be projected from historical experience.

It is trite to observe that data and information are not the same. However, having a practical definition of how they differ can be extremely helpful. Many definitions exist in the literature, but we would like to suggest some that are particularly useful in this context.

Simply put, *data* is a physical quantification of historical phenomena, where even human activity (including thought) may be included. Because data is essentially physical, regardless of what medium it exists in, it requires that it be stored as a physical quantity or it ceases to exist. As a quantification of something historical, each datum may be accurate to a very high level of precision or it may be inaccurate to the point of being false. Any set of data may or may not be usable or may have no value, which is to say either it contains no information or we do not, at the moment, have the means to extract information from it. Moreover, data may even contain misinformation, as any data set may include errors or other deficiencies, known or unknown. One definition of information is that it consists of facts that are approximate, but for which *the probabilistic characteristics of their accuracy have been established.* Information is, by this definition, usable and valuable. But value and usefulness are not simply qualities that information possesses, in the way that an object has color or shape. Information is usable and valuable because the process of information creation is teleological—information is always created for a purpose: *to be used.*

Working Definitions

Data: A physical quantification of historical phenomena. It typically exists in significant volume. It is typically infused with error.

Information: Facts that are approximate, and forecasts of future events, for which *the probabilistic characteristics of their accuracy have been established.*

Model: A mechanism that estimates an unknown quantity, or establishes the probabilistic characteristics, of data or functions of data.

We might wish to kick the tires of these definitions with some simple examples to see how well they hang together. For example, we might consider whether or not there is overlap. Are data elements themselves information? Consider the data presented in Figure 3.2: hourly air temperatures for the city of Madrid. These data elements

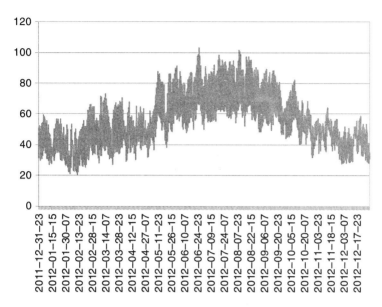

Figure 3.2 Air Temperature in Madrid (Fahrenheit)
Data Source: www.weathermetrics.com

were stored, as most computer-stored data are, as physical binary digital values. As the quantification of historical phenomena, they certainly meet our data definition. But if we ask ourselves whether any given datum is a fact, we will quickly be led down a path requiring an infinity of supporting information in order to establish that any data point can elevated to that status of fact. Is it a fact that at midnight on December 31, 2012, it was 29.5 degrees Fahrenheit in Madrid? Someone has claimed it to be so. But could it have been the same temperature in all parts of Madrid? The number must either represent a measurement at a single location (with some consequent level of uncertainty as to what temperatures were being experienced in other parts of the city), or it is some average over multiple locations (with some other, perhaps lower, level of uncertainty as to what tempera-tures were being experienced in other parts of the city). Probably too, the measurement instruments themselves are subject to some level of measurement error. And what precisely is the geographical definition of Madrid associated with these data? And so on.

Were we to study in detail the questions raised above, we might then be able to characterize the probabilistic accuracy of that specific data point, at which point we could call it both a fact, and information, by our definition. The degree to which the probabilistic characteristics of data need to be understood to convert them into information depends in part on the intended use to which the information will be put.

The above definitions of data and information follow from the well-trodden philosophical ground frequently associated with the observations of Popper[5] (and others) that all knowledge is conjectural, and that what we are calling *information* is subjective in nature. Taken seriously, all analysis—including statistical analysis—is also subjective. Here we are simply saying that we may draw a line, and elevate so-called facts that can be supported with enough statistical analysis (however subjective such analysis may be) to characterize the accuracy of the fact probabilistically, to a special status of usefulness and label that *information*. Let us take this one step further. Suppose we have a separate interest in the average temperature in Madrid. We may be considering using a construction material designed specifically to perform well under widely varying temperatures, but whose overall longevity is a function of the average temperature to which it is exposed, and we need that average to make that choice. The data set in Figure 3.2 contains 8,784 observations, with an average of 53.78 degrees. The 8,784 data points form an empirical distribution from which we can recover standard deviations, quantile ranges, or any statistic we require to characterize the temperature distribution *as a probability distribution*, even though it is a subjective choice for us to make this leap. Under mild additional assumptions, we can appeal to the central limit theorem to quantify the uncertainty in the quantity of interest—the 53.78. It is the standard error, in this case 0.175 of one degree. With this piece of information we could be comfortable labeling the average temperature as information. To return to the EUT discussion in Chapter 1, we can see that in using these definitions, that although the contents of an institution's 31 million spreadsheets is certainly data, much of this data could not feasibly be converted into information, or would not be worth the conversion were it feasible.

Before leaving this topic it should be pointed out that many other views of these concepts and associated definitions of terms exist, even within the literature of corporate management and institutional organization. Included among these is the view that information is purely a mental concept—that it exists only as an instantaneous state of perception within the human mind. Under this view, data is defined largely by how it is stored and processed. Raw data and the outputs of statistical models are of an equivalent nature. Both are sets of numbers to be stored in a database, and charted, examined, or further processed to (hopefully) turn into information as they are mentally consumed by their audiences. Another view elevates knowledge over information, and in a full-circle distancing from Popper, equates knowledge with belief.[6] In this form of radical subjectivism, one can organize data processing strategies any way one believes is appropriate without reference to design principles, or even abandon strategy altogether and let the organization evolve as it may, since any outcome for the firm might be the best.

DATA QUALITY

Data quality control, particularly in the financial services industry, is gradually crystallizing into a discipline with accepted definitions and practices. It is now widely understood that the amount and quality of information that can be created is a function of the amount and quality of the data available to support information creation. As such, data can be viewed as a productive asset whose productivity may be a function of quality.[7] This section discusses data quality from an applied practice perspective, but it is worth noting that an institution intending to view data as a productive asset will need to ensure that the organizational structure has data ownership built in as a key function and aligned with the rest of the data processing personnel as described in Chapter 2. A comprehensive data inventory and associated data definitions, as well as the details of data ownership, ought to be widely communicated so that users know what data is available and who the specific owners of the data they use are, especially if the data owners hold the responsibility for the quality of their data and for managing data quality control processes. Effective data inventorying and clarity of ownership also helps enables a more effective wing-to-wing model validation function, as discussed further in Chapter 4.

Commonly used definitions of data quality include four distinct characteristics of data that can be separately measured and monitored: completeness, conformity, validity, and accuracy.[8] *Completeness* means whether the data that is expected to exist actually does exist. This means both that there are no missing rows in the data and that there are no missing field values. The latter can be evaluated by query with a simple NULL check, although such a test must be applied field by field. The former is more challenging, may require significant effort to assess, and may only be possible to evaluate probabilistically. *Conformity* refers to whether the contents conform to specific characteristics (such as whether each zip code consists of five digits) and since these characteristics can be described as rules the tests are also easily applied by query-as-rule tests. *Validity* relates to quality at the data class or data field level. Continuing with the zip code example, a validity measure would test the frequency with which field values appear to be valid zip codes based on some authoritative reference table, in this case a complete set of postal codes provided by the U.S. Postal Service. This flags *conforming* but not *valid* codes, such as 99999. While validity tests are also easily performed by query, they typically need some reference data that may not be structured identically to the data being tested, and so some thought may need to be applied to implement the test. *Accuracy* relates to the correctness of each specific field level value: For example, "Is John Doe's zip code 08540?" To answer this question for a bulk data set (as opposed to a single name) there are three possible tactics:

1. Employ an authoritative reference data set.
2. Research each data element through alternative means.
3. Employ data profiling techniques.

The first tactic is the best, since it can be automated and can be highly (if not fully) comprehensive. In fact, this approach is embedded in (or more accurately, unnecessary in) the centralized integrated data model, augmented with a strategic data acquisition function. That is, if an authoritative reference data set exists within the system, all data containing the field in question should be derived directly from that authoritative source, ensuring the accuracy of all downstream manifestations of this data element. If the most authoritative version of the data that is furthest upstream is believed to contain errors, that situation could be remediated by reference to an *external* authoritative reference source. Then steps should be taken to acquire that data as the system source, eliminating all downstream errors once and for all. To visualize this, consider the two diagrams in Figures 3.1 and 3.2. In Figure 3.1 it is clear that data quality control processes should be located all the way to the left, targeting only data stored in the central repository. From this position there is no risk that quality controls will be applied only to a subset of the data and all downstream users of the data will benefit from them. In Figure 3.2, however, there are three possible locations for data quality processes (at least): at the source systems on the left, within the data hub in the center, or at data marts emanating from the hub on the right. Each of these carries some risk that the controls will be applied only to a subset of the data, since other similar data elements might exist elsewhere in the system. This lack of certainty that existing data quality controls have been applied universally can create incentives for local end users to perform their own data quality controls—and possibly local remediations.

Whatever the system architecture, researching data by alternative means tends to be very costly and time consuming, and is effective only if the volume of data to be remediated is low and efficient means to research the data exist. This in turn depends in part on the approach the firm is taking to identify data errors, discussed further in the chapter. This method is probably most often used and most effective in responding piecemeal to discovered errors. For example, when bills or account statements mailed out to customers are returned by the postal service, researchers can call or e-mail customers directly to correct addresses. Or, when gross reconciliation errors are traced to erroneous information in an underlying account system, manual researching of the account activity may be used to correct the error. Obviously, this is a costly and reactive approach that can only form a small part of an effective data quality program.

Data profiling is both an art and a science, through which an institution can inspect data proactively through a variety of techniques that range from visual inspection of data plots by subject matter experts all the way to sophisticated modeling that seeks to predict data from other data and then focuses attention on the data points for which the prediction accuracy is low. As an example of the first type of data pro-filing, a national service provider with significant market share might presume (or have determined through sample testing) that its cus-tomer base is roughly proportional to population; say, 8 to 10 percent of the population. By visually inspecting the customer count as a per-centage of their overall customer base superimposed on the population percentage as published by the Census Bureau it could identify possi-ble systemic data errors, and this could be done at state, county, MSA, city, or local level as required. For an example of the second type—the model-based approach to profiling—consider an insurance company with clean and rich customer data. It may be possible for it to use mul-tivariate customer data to predict what types of coverage the customer is likely to purchase. Then, by matching actual coverage with predicted coverage, those observations with poor matches can be examined to determine whether either the coverage data or the customer data has any error. Model-based data-quality evaluation tools are extremely powerful because they can be largely automated and can be improved and tuned over time to detect better and to avoid false positives. While visual inspection may seem like the least sophisticated approach in this spectrum, properly deployed it can be the most powerful. The informed human mind is the most powerful pattern-recognition tool available, and visual inspection of basic data plots can immediately reveal not only outlier problems or distributional problems, but other anoma-lies that even a well-programmed computer would certainly miss. This process is easier than ever to implement using powerful new data visu-alization tools that connect directly to source data structures. Given the level of institutional risk that can result from gross errors in key data elements and the ease with which visual inspection can be performed, it should be incorporated into the overall data quality program as both a role and a responsibility.

An illustrative anecdote may characterize the risks that may result from a failure to critically inspect key data elements. In the late 1990s a large North American institution acquired a large bank domiciled in another country. As part of the integration, a data integration program was launched that involved, among other things, visual inspection of the acquired bank's data. In a data set of commercial loans that spanned more than a decade, it was observed that there was an impossible concentration of defaults occurring in October of 1996—more than 75 percent of all defaults occurred in that month. The acquired bank acknowledged this as an error: A database *load date* had inadvertently been written into the *default date* field. This error was not recoverable, except through manual review of hundreds of paper files. While the error produced a costly loss of information, the fact that the error had been identified was a great risk mitigant to the acquiring institution. At about the same time, a major software vendor released with some fanfare a credit model designed specifically for use in the country of the acquired bank. The acquired bank had been a partner in the development of this model and a major supplier of data. In the vendor's published report detailing the development and performance of the model, a remarkable chart was exhibited—a history of defaults in that country showing that nearly 50 percent of all defaults occurred in October of 1996! Obviously, no attempt had been made to predict default dates from the macro and obligor data used in the model and to compare them to the empirical dates, or the error would have been discovered. Embarassingly, the data also had not been visually inspected, either during the development of the model or prior to publishing the report.

As Herzog et al. explain,[9] there are three things an institution can do to address poor data quality:

1. Prevention: Keep bad data out of the database.
2. Detection: Proactively search for bad data already present in the system.
3. Repair: Let the bad data reveal itself through use and then fix it.

To employ the first method, an institution must have strong control over all of the data entry points into the system. This is another compelling reason not only to have a centralized data storage model, but also to treat data acquisition as a strategic function and staff it accordingly. As with the first method, the second method can be performed with much greater efficiency and permanence if it can be applied once over a centralized data core; it also needs to be supported by strong prevention. Obviously every institution will be stuck doing some data repair, but the proportion an institution allocates to each of these three methods should be largely under its control, although perhaps constrained by system design limitations that can only be addressed longer term. Herzog et al. suggest that for U.S. firms (in all industries), the typical mix of data quality efforts is on the order of

- Prevent (10 percent)
- Detect (30 percent)
- Repair (60 percent)

While the authors' recommendation from a cost-effectiveness perspective (even without the benefit of the centralized fully-integrated architecture) is

- Prevent (45 percent)
- Detect (30 percent)
- Repair (25 percent)

Here, the old adage about prevention and cure could be restated as "550 kilobytes of prevention is worth 1 megabyte of cure." Certainly, with a fully centralized model the recommended allocations would have to be skewed even further in the direction of prevention. In Chapter 3 of Herzog et al.'s excellent book, the authors discuss data quality as something that should be treated strategically and that can produce direct competitive advantages, citing five illustrative cases of U.S. firms generating direct competitive benefits through targeted data quality (although not in the financial services sector).

As the foregoing discussion serves to highlight, another key benefit of the centralized data model, augmented with a data acquisition function, is that the strategy and tactics for a data quality assurance, or enterprise data quality (EDQ), function can be straightforwardly designed to align with that structure. More specifically, when data is stored centrally and then brought to users through organized stages of denormalization and logical data views, the place to locate the kind of data testing described above is clear and obvious—all the way upstream. By placing the data quality work at the source, the quality of all of the data in the system will be known, the work will only need to be done once, and all users will benefit from, and can be informed of this critical work. In addition, the prioritization and sequencing of the data quality work stream can be driven by the known uses of the data and can be recoverable from the known structure by informed personnel deployed as in Figure 2.3 with the full range of anticipated data acquisitions (which should be planned and prioritized, as discussed further later).

Historically, institutions could not take advantage of this highly efficient data quality approach for two reasons. First, they typically do not have sufficiently centralized data models. Consequently they apply data quality programs at multiple locations throughout the system, often driven by particular and narrowly identified quality needs or concerns. Tying this back to our discussion in Chapter 2, when the firm permits a proliferation of data marts serving specialized uses, including those that act as entry points for certain data, the firm creates the need for multiple, often duplicative, data quality work streams. This of course means that some data quality work may be redundant as separate users of like data seek to have their own data quality needs met. Even worse, some users of data that has (so to speak) flowed off the main route may not benefit from any of this work and may be using poor quality versions of data, when better, remediated versions of the data exist elsewhere. Also, because data quality is essentially an analytic function, that is, *one that also requires expertise in the analytic uses of data*, firms have been forced to locate data quality work as close to the analytic layer as possible since that is where the capable human resources are located. In other words, *in performing a task whose efficiency is maximized by locating the work as far upstream as possible, institutions are only able to accomplish it by locating the work as far downstream as possible*!

MODELS AND THEIR ROLE

Practically speaking, and given our definitions, information is typically created when data is used to answer a question.[10] Simple examples include: What is the average temperature in Madrid? How does the loss accumulation rate differ under recessionary versus expansionary economic environments? How much could we sell this asset for? In such cases, a model (of some kind) is a required effect of that conversion. Sometimes the question being asked is basic enough that the answer required is a simple fact. In these cases a model is not required to produce the answer even though the answer is derived from data, and these cases have as their distinguishing feature that the answer to the question is itself more data. What were total sales for the quarter? How many countries are we operating in? How much exposure do we have to Enron? But while the answers to these basic questions inform, it is in support of decision making—*choice under uncertainty*—that models are needed to produce the information that informs. And the higher the volume of data that we have at our disposal, or the more complex the question, the more dependent we are on models to extract the needed information.

As is the case with financial institutions themselves, the definition of *models* involves thorny boundary problems. While it may be fairly straightforward to identify things that are not models, this process of elimination does little to address the question of what constitutes a unit of observation within the model space. It is a common practice to bundle together multiple analytic tools and call the assembled tool a model. Such multifunction analytic systems can be huge—so huge and so dynamic that they are impossible to validate or risk-assess as a unit, even though they may be called models. For example, Black-rock's Aladdin system, which performs a host of asset management functions, is often called a model, even though it performs a multiplic-ity of functions and is reported to have over 25 million lines of code that are subject to ongoing revisions.[11]

Another pitfall to be avoided is the use of the term *model* to describe something that's only a methodology or technique, net of specific parameters or fitting to actual data. It may seem obvious that ordinary least squares should not be called a model while a specific ordinary least squares (OLS) regression should. However, some institutions employ modeling platforms to handle repetitive modeling tasks and look to simplify governance and risk assessment by referring to (and sometimes validating) such a platform as the model, with specific output-producing results as inheriting their validity from the validity of the platform. To avoid the conceptual quagmires that such practices would engender, we will restrict our use of the word *model* to refer to narrowly focused actual implementations of analytic tools designed to produce specific outputs for specific purposes.

Models characterize data with respect to expectations, variances, and its relationship to other data. They also characterize any number of quantitative and qualitative features of the data. In simple terms, a model is a mechanism to convert data into information, or to combine data with other information to produce enriched and more focused information. This simple definition can be shown to be practical, particularly when compared to popular alternatives. Moreover, this definition explains both what a model is and what its role is. Within financial institutions, the definition of a model has recently been the subject of a lot of hand-wringing, as firms contemplated compliance with regulatory requirements for model governance and model validation. In particular, this definition squares well with the Fed's definition from SR 11-7:

> ... the term *model* refers to a quantitative method, system, or approach that applies statistical, economic, financial, or mathematical theories, techniques, and assumptions to process input data into quantitative estimates. A *model* consists of three components: an information input component, which delivers assumptions and data to the model; a processing component, which transforms inputs into estimates; and a reporting component, which translates the estimates into useful business information.

The last phrase, "useful business information," highlights the fact that business decisions are based on information as defined. More information allows for more informed decision making, and although it would be a stretch to conclude that more informed decisions are better decisions in every case, it is less controversial to assert that poor business decisions can usually be associated with decision makers who were poorly informed. For financial institutions, it is increasingly through the use of models that decision makers become informed. It is difficult to list more than a few key business decision-making processes that do not depend significantly on models to supply critical information. From underwriting to asset selection and management to product development and business strategy all the way to capital management and business development, models are more and more heavily used. It is then self-evident that better models, fed by more, better quality, and more timely data, can provide decision makers with better information and an advantaged position relative to their peers.

Consider the range of financial services whose success depends on informed decision making and whose foundation is a supply of information that depends crucially on models. These services include the pricing of insurance policies, the setting of interest rates and fees on deposits, marketing and product design, the valuation of assets, the structuring of complex credit products, asset risk hedging, the setting of risk tolerances and limits (both for assets and for liabilities), anti-money laundering and fraud detection, asset/liability and liquidity management, stress testing, economic capital modeling, and the application of portfolio optimization theory. More could be cited, and of course most of the areas listed require many interconnected modeling disciplines and applications, not just one.

Clearly, then, most of the key functions of any financial institution are model-dependent and the role of these models is to produce information to be used by decision makers. Importantly, decision makers cannot do their jobs effectively if they are simply presented with model outputs labeled generically as *information*. It is the job of the analytics function not only to produce and communicate model outputs but also to understand and communicate the quantity and quality of the information content of those model outputs. This is not an easy task, since the job requires the analysts both to communicate technical and often subtle information to a less technical audience and carefully measure and monitor the information content of their model outputs—a discipline rarely pursued in the financial services sector (although more common in other higher risk/reward industries like pharmaceuticals). Broadly, one can think of the provision of information to decision makers as the point at which information is brought over the finish line. Given that most of the value of the data and analytic infrastructure is created at this point, the characterization and communication of the information content of model outputs at this critical point can determine how much value has truly been created. This communication is important not only from the perspective of informed decision making but also (as we will discuss further later) from a resource allocation perspective, since presumably the qualitative or quantitative aspects of the information content of any model's output could be improved through the application of additional resources.

A Classic Example: Probability of Default Models

Let's consider an example of a type of model-based information creation using a model class ubiquitous within financial institutions and widely used for a variety of key decisions—the class of models that estimate probabilities of default (PDs) for corporate obligors. We saw from Table 1.1 in Chapter 1 that firm practices and results in this model class vary widely. And, using our definitions above, it may seem as if PDs don't even qualify as information, since they are not forecasts of future events and, even if their probabilistic characteristics are known, they are not approximate facts. However, this apparent contradiction derives from the use of the term probability, not from our definition of information. As is well known by statisticians and choice theorists, there exist two separate concepts of probability with separate analytical paradigms: case probability and subjective probability. Under the former, from which the theory of statistics arises, the term probability refers to the properties associated with a mapping from a fixed state space to a fixed outcome set. Under this framework, the crucial assumption on which the framework is based is *repeatability*. Obviously for unique historical (and future) events, the repeatability assumption does not apply. Under the latter concept, the term probability refers to a mental assessment of likelihood. This assessment process is what underlies human choice in cases in which the repeatability assumption does not apply—or worse, and more commonly—when *the entire causal mechanism that will ultimately produce the outcome is unknown or poorly understood*. This is radical uncertainty to Knight[12] and sheer ignorance to Kirzner.[13] The process of likelihood assessment (and choice) under radical uncertainty would not be very evolved were it not for the fact that strong patterns can often be observed in the real world, in spite of the inapplicability of the repeatability assumption—hence the strong value-add of models.

In the case of corporate default strong patterns certainly do exist, and some cases, such as the repeated bankruptcy filings of Marvel Entertainment and AMF Bowling, make one scratch one's head and wonder if the repeatability assumption may have limited applicability. Ultimately then, the corporate PD concept is really a pattern recognition concept, which can be translated into a subjective probability depending on one's belief in the strength of the identified pattern. That is, whether or not a given firm will default over the next 12 months will only be revealed through the passage of time, and today's PD cannot mean anything other than that a pattern has been discovered wherein *firms like this* have historically defaulted at a rate of x percent.[14] Clearly, then, it falls to the analysts to ensure that decision makers who use PDs understand fully the meaning of this particular class of model output. In practice, the patterns that can be established in historical corporate default experience are typically identified using a variety of data including financial statement information, equity prices (where available), payment behavior and other observed behavior. These are models. Frequently, creditworthiness indicators (typically agency ratings or commercial credit bureau scores), which are themselves nothing more than pattern recognition models, are also included, so that *models based on models* are now common. As we stated at the beginning of this section, the role of models is to convert data into information, or to combine data with other information to produce enriched and more focused information. Vendor models that produce or purport to produce corporate PDs abound, with widely varying coverage and widely varying performance.

Beyond all of the indicators of creditworthiness discussed above, patterns of default behavior cannot be identified without actual default observations that can be included in the data set. Since corporate default rates typically average between 2 and 4 percent depending on the sample, these default observations are high-leverage points, which is to say they are *information laden* and so have a very high value. Any institution engaged in extending commercial credit should place a premium on effectively capturing all of its internal default data in a way that facilitates linking it to customer data, transactional data, and all of the available creditworthiness data that could be used for pattern recognition. In addition, it may be beneficial to acquire external default data to augment the internal flow. For years rating agencies have been the premier providers of electronic default data, but their universe is restricted to entities with bond ratings, only a small fraction of the commercial borrowing pool. In the age of the Internet and unlimited data capture, a wide variety of options exist for financial institutions to acquire key data elements (such as corporate default event data) and integrate them into their data systems. A small effort in this particular area can pay huge dividends in terms of information gain. So the question to be asked and answered by each financial institution is, "How much is an increment of information enrichment for my PDs worth, and how much does it cost?" Importantly, the question of how much an incremental unit of information is worth should be evaluated not simply as the value that accrues to the marginal transaction, but rather with respect to its longer term effect on profitability and competitiveness in and across all of the activities for which PDs may be used. This case is instructive, because the PDs may be used in a wide range of activities, including underwriting, pricing, and approval authority for commercial lending; credit limits and capital allocation; credit hedging and securities trading; structuring and pricing of credit derivatives such as CDOs; and stress testing and regulatory compliance.

Other Examples

Another instructive example is that of loss reserving. The reserving processes and regulatory requirements around reserving are quite different in banks versus insurance companies. For insurance products, statutory reserves are required to cover the full embedded loss (payouts) in the existing (in force) policy portfolio. For some products (such as life insurance) this means estimating mortality rates over long future time periods: 30 years or more in many cases. Small changes in mortality estimates can have large implications for future losses. While historical mortality rates are remarkably stable (at least with respect to some known trends; e.g., people tend to live longer over time), certain factors could have major impacts on forward rates, and these need to be modeled probabilistically. These factors include things such as pandemic potential (possibly estimated by country or region), medical advances that could reduce mortality rates from specific diseases, and environmental factors (such as ozone depletion and global warming). Because any of these phenomena could have long-term effects, they all have the potential to drive large changes in total embedded loss and hence current reserves. As such, these forward-looking probabilistic models can directly drive key balance sheet items, even with all of the regulatory controls and requirements that such statistics are subject to. Reserve model changes (even improvements) must therefore be carefully managed, as they represent the lens through which investors, counterparties, customers, and regulators will view the firm.

At the other end of the spectrum are probability models, which are used to establish the probabilities of (assumed) very low probability events, or to characterize properties of unlikely (tail) events. Economic capital models and other VaR (value at risk) models fall into this class. For models whose focus is on the characterization of extreme tail events, it is obviously difficult or impossible to evaluate the outputs against observed actual values. This makes it exceedingly difficult to test or measure the value of the information being produced. In such cases subjective assessment is usually the best that can be done, and the focus has to be on the conceptual design of the model and the transparency and intuition of its assumptions. In addition, the integrity of the entire process that supports the modeling must be carefully assessed—more so than for models whose performance can be gauged directly from observable outcomes. As one team of practitioners responsible for evaluating complex ECAP (economic capital) models observed,

> Within a financial institution, a [complex portfolio] model requires mathematics, numerical algorithms, data processing code, data systems and hardware, and people trained to create and assemble all of these parts. The greatest single mitigant of model risk is a culture in which a heightened sensitivity to model risk is shared across the risk team.[15]

Models and the Value of Information Creation

As can be seen from the preceding examples and many others, almost any conversion of data into information is performed using a model. Many models create information directly from empirical data by providing the probabilistic characteristics of approximate facts, as per our definition. For example, even a simple average is a model—which can be described as a regression model where the dependent variable is the function $f(x) = 1$. But (again referring to our definition), while a reported average by itself is merely data, an average (along with its associate minimum and maximum, or standard deviation, or whatever probabilistic characteristic is needed to answer a specific question) is information. We typically refine our questions by placing additional conditions within them. And for every incrementally conditioned question, a more sophisticated model with more embedded conditioning is required to produce an answer. Importantly, the measurement of the accuracy of that conditioned output needs to include some measure of that additional complexity for the answers to be truly informative. For econometricians this is standard practice; if not obvious, at least embedded in the techniques of regression and time series diagnostics. In particular, statistics such as the adjusted R-squared and the Akaike information criterion measure the benefit of improved in-sample fit weighed against the cost of potential overfitting due to insufficient data or due to excess conditioning. For actuaries, sample data is often evaluated using a credibility index, which assesses the signal to noise ratio in the sample and hence can be used to establish a priori whether or not a model can be supported based on the sample in question. Credibility measures, however, do not assess the information content of a particular model, and so are of less direct value in this context.

For information generating processes within a business context, and the communication of model generated results, the same principles should apply. That is, whenever information is being presented in support of a decision-making process, it should be presented along with information on how much conditioning was done and how much residual uncertainty remains. For example, if statistical peer comparisons are being used to inform senior leaders about a potential strategic marketing endeavor, the analysis may (within limits) be more robust if more relevant peer data is used. However, the variance of the key statistics may rise or fall with the inclusion/exclusion of specific peers. For the analysis to be truly informative, the sensitivities to changes in the peer cohort should be carefully analyzed and presented along with the mean and variance statistics typically deemed to be of primary importance. Within an institution, users of model-generated information will have different levels of training and different levels of appetite for such detailed statistical diagnostics. Therefore, a useful simplifying tool is to create a model risk index that can be used as a proxy for such diagnostics and against which different types of models on a comparable basis can be placed for comparison. Such an approach is discussed further in Chapter 4.

Beyond the simple conversion of data into information, higher levels of information (including estimates of unknown quantities and forecasts of future events) can be created from existing information (often by adding additional data), as long as those quantities can be effectively characterized probabilistically. Predictive modeling goes further than merely characterizing facts embedded in empirical data, and looks to forecast future events, prices, and patterns of behavior. As we observed from surveying the model dependent processes within financial institutions, predictive modeling is one of the disciplines through which much of the competitive advantage of information processing occurs. A 2013 Towers Watson survey of North American property and casualty insurers revealed that insurance firms are

> ... keenly aware that predictive modeling offers a competitive advantage. At least 85 percent reported a positive impact on rate accuracy, nearly 80 percent on profitability, and at least 74 percent on loss ratios.[16]

Banks and other financial institutions face similar impact ratios. It is probably fair to say that most of the important modeling that financial institutions do is predictive. As we have observed already, since this means that institutions' future financial performance is dependent on today's effective predictive modeling, market participants have become increasingly sensitive to the presence of model risk, both within institutions and across the financial system. Among those expressing concern about model risk has been the regulatory community, and we survey some of the ways it has expressed that concern and sought to address it at this point in the chapter.

REGULATORY REGIMES AND GUIDANCE

As discussed previously, the subject of model risk has become increasingly important as market participants have become increasingly cognizant of the fact that advanced modeling underlies more and more of the innovation in the financial services industry and represents the front line with respect to how institutions compete. In spite of that, much of the activity within financial institutions that could be called model risk management is being driven less by the competitive advantage that might be gained by reducing model risk and more by the guidelines and minimum requirements set by regulators. In this section we consider some of the specific regulations and regulatory guidance with the aim of interpreting their underlying messages and gauging the extent to which commercial and regulatory objectives could be aligned.

SR 11-7

A lot of the current furor in the U.S. financial services industry over model governance stems from Federal Reserve memo SR 11-7 and its predecessor OCC 2011-12, "Sound Practices for Model Risk Management," which itself replaced OCC 2000-16, published in May of 2000, eight years before the crisis of 2008. At 21 pages, SR 11-7 and OCC 2011-12 are virtually identical and quite terse, so U.S. regulatory guidance on model risk management is neither ambiguous nor hard to find or understand. While guidance was originally intended for banks specifically, extension of the Fed regulatory regime to SIFIs under Dodd-Frank brought insurance companies and nonbank financial institutions under the regulatory framework and effectively established a standard for the industry as a whole.

The standards and requirements set forth in SR 11-7 are essentially minimum prudential standards for managing models within an institution whose performance (and perhaps survival) depends crucially on those models. The Fed itself has held and expressed this view. In two separate public talks in 2013, Karen Schneck, head of the Models and Methodologies Department at the New York Fed, explained how surprised the Fed teams were that institutions were balking at compliance with the guidance and complaining that it was too onerous and too costly to comply with. Schneck told listeners that the Fed had felt that the SR 11-7 document was largely reiterating existing guidance and expressing, in a concise way, those elements of good governance that most institutions should have already adopted and embraced. But at the time of this writing, few institutions can claim to be fully SR 11-7 compliant and many continue to wrestle mightily with some of its most basic components. Complaints that it's too far-reaching and prescriptive continue to be voiced.

The fact that financial institutions have been so ill-prepared to meet basic regulatory requirements[17] and the popularity of the idea that compliance with these requirements can be managed by narrowing the definition of what constitutes a model is symptomatic of the fact that financial institutions have been thinking about themselves and their core competencies in archaic and obsolete ways. A more modern approach to managing the institution overall, which would target a stronger competitive position and better financial performance, would put the firm in a position to govern and manage its model suite in ways that far exceed any regulatory requirements or expectations.

Basel II and Solvency II

So much has been written about the various Basel regimes that readers are likely on the threshold of topic fatigue. Topic fatigue notwithstanding, it may be worthwhile to quickly consider the extent to which the Basel directives are truly targeting—and the extent to which banks are actually struggling with—the enhancement of information processing capabilities.

The Basel regime, effectively published in 2004, is characterized as having three pillars:

Pillar I is a capital adequacy regime based on measures of credit risk, market risk, and operational risk.

Pillar II is a set of internal risk assessment standards that go beyond the three types of risk covered under Pillar I.

Pillar III is a set of disclosure requirements that augment standard positional and accounting disclosures with information generated using the Pillar II requirements.

Pillar I

While the stated goal of Pillar I is to ensure that banks maintain adequate minimum capital requirements based on the nature of their exposures, a strong incentive is embedded in the rules that directly targets banks' information processing capabilities. The incentive stems from the multiple regimes included under the rules. Pillar I identifies three approaches to calculating required capital—the standardized approach, the Foundation IRB approach, and the Advanced IRB approach—which are all associated with increasingly higher levels of capability with respect to data capture, data processing, and modeling. IRB stands for *internal ratings-based* and the approach is focused largely on credit risk. The idea behind the three regimes is that when firms can demonstrate more effective quantitative risk measurement, they can use that capability to adjust their capital to more closely match their risk profiles. The intention is that (in most cases) the coarser rule sets would require more capital, creating a profit incentive for institutions to meet the requirements of the more sophisticated model-based regimes.

In following the voluminous commentary and debate on the sequential capital regimes, it appears that there is a presumption (among regulators, academics, and bank managers) that smaller institutions will be able to compete in the marketplace with the higher capital requirements imposed under the less sophisticated approaches and the lower costs associated with lower modeling and information processing capabilities. Part of this may reflect the antiquated view that better modeling capabilities are primarily useful for meeting regulatory requirements, not for driving improved financial performance, and that underinvestment in these capabilities is preferable whenever regulatory requirements can be avoided. Given the discussion in Chapter 1 about the patterns of entry and exit in the U.S. banking sector, such a strategy seems fraught with risk.

Pillar II

Pillar II is also known as the Internal Capital Adequacy Assessment Program, or ICAAP. There are many descriptions and summaries of ICAAP, but the one from the Canadian Office of the Superintendent of Financial Institutions serves our purpose well:

A rigorous ICAAP has six main components:

1. Board and senior management oversight
2. Sound capital assessment and planning

3. Comprehensive assessment of risks

4. Stress testing

5. Monitoring and reporting

6. Internal control review

While these fundamental features of ICAAP are broadly prescribed, there is no single "correct" approach, and one approach does not fit all institutions. An institution's ICAAP should be as simple or complex as needed, and should reflect how the institution is managed and organized in practice. It should not be established solely to fulfill a regulatory requirement.[18]

Each of these six components rests solidly on a foundation of information processing, and none can be accomplished well without excellence in data and information processing. With the exception of the planning element of the second component, which can be argued to have more to do with entrepreneurial vision, all of these items can be seen as explicit directives to meet examiners' expectations with respect to specific features of a bank's information processing complex. Even the planning element of component two is squarely tied to the production of information, since even the most visionary entrepreneurs need facts and other information to form their view of the future.

Perhaps most important is the last sentence of the guidance. This is an unambiguous statement of a theme that pervades much of the recent regulatory language, across regulators, countries, and sectors of the financial services industry. The theme is that regulators feel compelled to establish requirements *and then instruct that they should not be met "solely to fulfill a regulatory requirement."* The implication is brutally stark: regulators do not believe financial institutions are doing the things that are in their own best interest, and their dissatisfaction is primarily focused on institutions' poor capabilities and low investment in information processing.

Pillar III

That demands for greater disclosure of risk information, much of it model-based, are intended at least in part to raise the standards and capabilities of banks in this area is straightforward. But at a broader level, regulators are clearly trying to establish a link between competitive advantage and excellence in information processing (much as this book is). By signaling that enhanced information flows are designed to benefit investors and customers alike (in addition to bank examiners), regulators are seeking to increase public demand for such information to the point where stock prices and market shares will be affected by institutions' relative performance. In case this motivation had not been fully obvious to market participants in the first 10 years of its existence, the BIS (Bank for International Settlements) reemphasized it in June 2014, saying

> Market discipline has long been recognized as a key objective of the Basel Committee on Banking Supervision. The provision of meaningful information about common key risk metrics to market participants is a fundamental tenet of a sound banking system. It reduces information asymmetry and helps promote comparability of banks' risk profiles within and across jurisdictions. Pillar 3 of the Basel framework aims to promote market discipline through regulatory disclosure requirements. These requirements enable market participants to assess more effectively key information relating to a bank's regulatory capital and risk exposures in order to instill confidence about a bank's exposure to risk and overall regulatory capital adequacy.[19]

The word *information* appears three times in this key paragraph. The Committee's attention appears to be focused on providing more and better information for depositors[20] and investors. As we discuss further in Chapter 6, these are just two of a larger set of key information flows through which financial institutions can generate competitive advantage.

Solvency II

Solvency II is a revised regulatory regime for European insurance companies, adopted by the Council of the European Union and the European Parliament in November 2009 and scheduled for implementation in January 2016. The regime is quite similar in spirit to Basel II and is described as resting on essentially the same three pillars, although the concept of pillars is not mentioned in the directive itself. Like Basel II, part of the goal is to create incentives for firms to develop better internal capital modeling capabilities. The two explicitly stated goals for the program are (1) greater consumer protection through more uniform and transparent standards, and (2) modernized supervision, which shifts supervisors' focus from compliance monitoring and rule-based capital requirements to evaluating insurers' risk profiles and the quality of their risk management and governance systems. The second stated goal is telling: The old-school regulatory capital regimes, in contrast, basically said once we've summarized a firm's risk, we can calculate how much capital they need to hold. Now the question has evolved to recognize the challenges and uncertainties involved in assessing and summarizing a firm's risk profile. The focus is now less on the measurement of the risk itself and more on firms' abilities to measure risk—which is all about information processing.

In particular, much like Basel II, under Solvency II companies can either use the standard formula to calculate capital requirements or, if approved by their local supervisor, their own internal models. Naturally, the approval to use internal models will rest on the institution's ability to manage the components of its information processing infrastructure deemed relevant by the examiners. These will certainly include data quality, completeness, and relevance. They also include a range of model governance controls that include model development standards, documentation, testing, and implementation standards, as well as standards for independent validation and approval. So (like Basel II), while Solvency II is on its face a capital adequacy regime, it very deliberately seeks to incent insurance firms to enhance their modeling capabilities as a complement to *and under certain circumstances as a substitute for* holding additional capital, as a mitigant against systemic risk.

Comprehensive Capital Analysis and Review (CCAR)

Comprehensive Capital Analysis and Review (CCAR) is the Federal Reserve's post-crisis supervisory mechanism for assessing the capital adequacy of large, complex BHCs (bank holding companies) and other SIFIs. This regime began following the adoption of the capital plans rule in November 2011, which was effectively a replacement for the supervisory capital assessment program (SCAP) of 2009. Under this rule, all top-tier BHCs domiciled in the United States with assets of $50 billion or more are required to develop and submit annual capital plans to the Federal Reserve. Central to the stated requirements of CCAR is the performance of detailed stress tests that estimate the effects of specific stress scenarios on the institution's capital and income. Minimum standards must be met for certain capital ratios even under these projected stressful conditions. But while CCAR appears on the surface to be directed toward systemic stability through the testing of capital adequacy during systemic stress, the roots of the approach and of the 2008 crisis suggest another compelling, if ulterior, motive. That is, capital adequacy aside, Fed requirements directly test institutions' information processing capabilities along multiple dimensions. Included in the 2011 document is this explicit program objective: "CCAR will provide the Federal Reserve with the information and perspective needed to help ensure that large bank holding companies have strong, firm-wide risk measurement and management processes supporting their internal assessments of capital adequacy."[21] Some notable CCAR failures and much of the direct criticism banks have received as a result of capital plan reviews have been directed at basic data and information weaknesses.

Supervisory dissatisfaction with banks' basic information processing capabilities was heightened through successive episodes that did not rise to the level of crisis but were nonetheless threatening: the Long-Term Capital Management (LTCM), Enron, and Parmalat failures in 2000, 2001, and 2003, respectively. In each of these situations, examiners concerned about the systemic effects repeatedly asked the same question of large banks: "What is your exposure to LTCM?," "What is your exposure to Enron?," "What is your exposure to Parmalat?" They rarely received satisfactorily quick or conclusive answers. Slightly more probing questions revealed that it was not simply exposure totals that were difficult to ascertain—the challenges often had more to do with banks' lack of ability to uniquely identify their customers, organize them into related corporate families, and effectively associate them with countries and industrial sectors. Recall from this chapter's earlier section, "Model Risk Mania," that these events were occurring just at the time that the Fed was formulating its organizational structure, scope, and approach to model governance. The Fed and other U.S. regulators were becoming concerned about the capabilities, accuracy, and controllership of basic data systems as well as key risk measurement systems. The latter included rating systems, PDs, and LGDs, where regulators were coming to recognize the magnitude of inconsistencies like those evidenced in the FSA studies presented in Table 1.1 in Chapter 1.

As a result, regulators began to look for ways to test and rate institutions' basic information processing capabilities, and bank solvency as well as systemic stability began to be seen as critically dependent on these capabilities as on capitalization. By 2009 a variety of indirect tests of information processing capabilities were embedded in the SCAP requirements. These included detailed data files that needed to be created, formatted, and delivered—data files that could be subjected to data profiling, consistency checks, or even reconciled among each other. The camel's nose was now under the data management and reporting tent, and banks did and continue to struggle to meet the new expectations for timely delivery of clean, accurate data and clean, sensible model outputs at the obligor and transaction level. Worse still, institutions with weak infrastructures often addressed CCAR requirements using processes that were massively spreadsheet-based. As a result Fed examiners experienced controllership shock, and through a tsunami of MRAs (matters requiring attention) helped to spawn the EUT control industry. Many of these institutions were forced to begin dismantling and replacing these brand-new spreadsheet-based processes after one or two cycles at a cost that can only be guessed at. Anecdotal evidence suggests that banks are about as likely to fail CCAR examinations on the basis of basic information processing deficiencies as they are to fail for inadequate capitalization. A Fed press release from March of 2014 announcing the results of the 2013 exams stated: "The Federal Reserve on Wednesday announced it has approved the capital plans of 25 bank holding companies participating in the Comprehensive Capital Analysis and Review (CCAR). The Federal Reserve objected to the plans of the other five participating firms—four based on qualitative concerns and only one because it did not meet a minimum post-stress capital requirement."[22]

The Sarbanes-Oxley Act (SOX)

The Sarbanes-Oxley Act of 2007 (SOX) served to provide investors and the general public with protection against fraudulent and erroneous representations of corporate performance by strengthening the requirements for corporate reporting and the penalties for misrepresentations of financial information and failure to comply with the law. For the purposes of this discussion, the material sections are 302, which establishes officer responsibilities for external disclosures, and 404, which requires the establishment and attestation of an appropriate control framework for protecting the information flow that supports such external disclosures. As such, SOX can be viewed as being primarily about data accuracy (although this includes some model outputs) and establishing responsibility for data accuracy as well as consequences for errors in disclosures as an enforcement mechanism. The Act applies to all public companies, not just financial institutions, but its message is straightforward: Legislators do not trust corporate leaders to ensure that public disclosures are accurate, whether based on willful intent to deceive or an inability to ensure quality. Certainly, Section 404 deals with the latter. The Act makes explicit the requirement that senior business leaders are able and willing to ensure that effective quality controls are in place to protect the accuracy of public disclosures had not been met.

As a result of SOX many firms were sent scrambling to establish new control mechanisms and in many cases new departments (SOX control departments), largely as overlays to their existing infrastructures and processes. As we have described above, when the core information processing complex is structurally flawed, such overlay approaches will provide control only at a very high cost. Those firms that can adapt their core infrastructure so that higher levels of control are inherent in the system may bear higher fixed costs to support those adaptations, but will enjoy better control at a lower cost going forward.

Principles-Based Reserving (PBR) for Insurance Products

The movement away from ad hoc and information-poor rule-based regulatory requirements and toward more information-rich model-based methods that we observed in bank capital regimes is being played out in many other areas within the broader financial services sector. An important area in which this trend is affecting practices and the competitive landscape is within the sphere of reserving and reserve requirements for a range of life insurance products. According to the National Association of Insurance Commissioners (NAIC),

> Reserve calculations for life insurance have been unchanged for almost 150 years. Currently, insurers use a formula-based static approach to calculate reserves for products. However, insurance products have increasingly grown in complexity, which led to a need for a new reserve method. The NAIC adoption of the Standard Valuation Law (SVL) in 2009 introduced a new method for calculating life insurance policy reserves. This new method, referred to as Principle-Based Reserving, or PBR, replaces the current formulaic approach to determining policy reserves with an approach that more closely reflects the risks of the highly complex products. The improved calculation is expected to "right-size reserves," reducing reserves that are too high for some products and increasing reserves that are too low for other products.[23]

And observers have described NAIC as being "in the midst of a concerted effort to introduce a new, principles-based system of reserving for life insurance and annuity products in the United States."[24] The evolution of actual reserve requirements has been somewhat product specific and closely linked to the pattern of product innovation. As products with unique risk features—including such products as universal life, and fixed and variable annuities with a plethora of technical features—were introduced, they (along with their respective reserve requirements) have typically been slotted into some preexisting category set up for regulatory purposes. However, as regulators struggled to ascertain what the true risks were in these liabilities they frequently observed that applied rules were ineffectively matched to the risks. Under the older approach, the solution would have been for regulators to craft and impose new reserve rules for each significant product innovation. With the rate of innovation increasing, this was clearly infeasible. Hence the PBR approach, with its emphasis on analytic rigor and reserve principles tied to analytic results, was born, and is now having an impact on policy and industry thinking across a wide range of life insurance products.

NOTES

1. Office of the Comptroller of the Currency (OCC), "Supervisory Guidance on Model Risk Management, OCC 2011-12" (2011): 1.
2. SIFI stands for *systemically important financial institution*, a designation created under the 2010 Dodd-Frank Act.
3. Financial Stability Board, "The Financial Crisis and Information Gaps" (October 29, 2009): 9, www.imf.org/external/np/g20/pdf/102909.pdf.
4. University of California, San Diego, "How Much Information?" 2009 Report on American Consumers," http://hmi.ucsd.edu/howmuchinfo_news_12_9_09.php.
5. Karl Popper, *Objective Knowledge: An Evolutionary Approach* (Oxford: Clarendon Press, 1972).
6. See, for example, Thomas H. Davenport and Laurence Prusak, *Working Knowledge: How Organizations Manage What They Know* (Boston: Harvard Business School Press, 1999).
7. This concept is discussed in more detail in Chapter 5.
8. Other, similar schemes are common in defining data quality. See, for example, Thomas N. Herzog, Fritz J. Scheuren, and William E. Winkler, *Data Quality and Record Linkage Techniques* (New York: Springer, 2007). Here the authors use five: relevance, accuracy, timeliness, comparability, and completeness—although they use these criteria for *databases* as well as data.
9. Ibid., 10–12.
10. Alternatively, information can be created from pure exploratory analysis.
11. Tracy Alloway, "BlackRock's Aladdin: Genie Not Included," *Financial Times*, July 7, 2014.
12. Frank H. Knight, Risk, *Uncertainty and Profit*, Boston, MA: Hart, Schaffner & Marx; Houghton Mifflin Company (1921).
13. Israel M. Kirzner, *The Meaning of Market Process: Essays in the Development of Modern Austrian Economics* (London: Routledge, 1975).
14. It is not germane to discuss so-called structural PD models here, except to say that they have been shown to be theoretically deficient, and that each implementation of such a model requires empirical calibration that pushes it back into the class of pattern recognition models, not case probability models.
15. Sean C. Keenan, Stefano Santilli, Sukyul Suh, Andrew Barnes, Huaiyu Ma, and Colin McCulloch, "Diversified Asset Portfolio Modelling: Sources and Mitigants of Model Risk," in *Model Risk: Identification, Measurement and Management*, eds. Harold Scheule and Daniel Rösch (London: Risk Books, 2010).

16. Towers Watson, *2013 Predictive Modeling Benchmarking Survey* (March 2014).

17. Both Federal Reserve memo SR 11-7 and its accompanying attachment can be found at www.federalreserve.gov/bankinforeg/srletters/sr1107.htm. As noted, other regulatory requirements apply to financial institutions as well.

18. OSFI, "Internal Capital Adequacy Assessment Process (ICAAP) for Deposit-Taking Institutions," Guideline E-19 (October 2010), www.osfi-bsif.gc.ca/Eng/fi-if/rg-ro/gdn-ort/gl-ld/Pages/icaap_dti.aspx#mozTocId942013.

19. BIS, Basel Committee on Banking Supervision, *Review of the Pillar 3 Disclosure Requirements* (June 2014).

20. For insurers, a policyholder would be a reasonable analogue to a bank depositor.

21. Board of Governors of the Federal Reserve System, "Comprehensive Capital Analysis and Review: Objectives and Overview" (March 18, 2011): 3.

22. Board of Governors of the Federal Reserve System, press release, March 16, 2013.

23. National Association of Insurance Commissioners, Center for Insurance Policy & Research, "Principles-Based Reserving," July 18, 2014, www.naic.org/cipr_topics/principle_based_reserving_pbr.htm.

24. Michael D. Devins and Michael K. McDonnell, *The Potential Impact of Principles-Based Reserving on Acquisitions and Divestitures in the Life Insurance Industry*, Debevoise & Plimpton Financial Institutions Report 4, no. 9 (October 2010): 1.

CHAPTER **4**

Model Risk
Measurement

As discussed in Chapter 3, model outputs become truly informative when they are communicated along with characterizations of their perceived accuracy or inaccuracy, as well as with other limitations of the model itself. Such characterizations are often highly technical, can be challenging to produce and communicate, and will vary across model types and classes. An institution can overcome some of these challenges and complexities and boost its information flow by developing a model risk measurement framework that can simply summarize the strengths and weaknesses of each model in a way that's easy for decision makers to understand. Reducing complex and heterogeneous model diagnostics into a simple and uniform index is not easy and many trade-offs and simplifications will be required to make such a system practical. But the payoffs should be great. Not only are decision makers better informed as a result, but resources may be more effectively allocated when the effect of relative and absolute improvement in model performance can be easily understood by management.

Certainly, financial institutions are being pushed toward greater capability in model risk assessment. A 2014 survey by a major consulting firm identified model risk measurement as a hot topic for banks and insurers. As we have already noted, this reflects a mixture of firms' interest in mitigating risk, particularly the type of headline risks that can curtail senior executive careers and embarrass boards, and direct pressure from regulators. As an example of the latter, Fed guidance requires CCAR filing institutions to include measures of model risk in their stress-testing results and overall capital planning. Such guidance was provided with the full knowledge that institutions were generally unprepared to produce such estimates with any amount of rigor, and that the industry as a whole was struggling with how to approach this topic. Part of this stems from the challenging nature of the problem itself. But certainly, part of it stems from the fact that the problem is far more challenging when the institution has poor information-processing capabilities generally. In this chapter, we provide some suggestions as to how firms might approach model risk measurement under the assumption that the firm has control over its broader information infrastructure, or at least is on a committed path toward that goal.

THREE PHASES OF MODEL MANAGEMENT

If a financial institution is able to set a strategy based on its assessment of its current and potential future competitive advantage, where information-processing capabilities form the core of that competitive advantage, it must be able to conduct that assessment quantitatively and with a significant amount of rigor. While data acquisition and processing form a foundation for those capabilities, it is the analytic layer and primarily the suite of models that the firm employs that will help to determine its competitive position. For most firms, reaching a state in which they can strategically assess their models and modeling capabilities requires passing through an evolutionary process that can be broken up into three distinct phases: a model governance phase, a model risk management phase, and an analytic asset management phase (see Figure 4.1). The goal is to be able to view individual models as assets, not merely in the sense that they are productive, but in the same sense as financial assets that can be assessed in terms of risk and return. This means having a quantitative measure of the asset's risk and the term structure of that risk, as well as having a quantitative assessment of the asset's expected return and the term structure of that return. Importantly, although there are significant dependencies

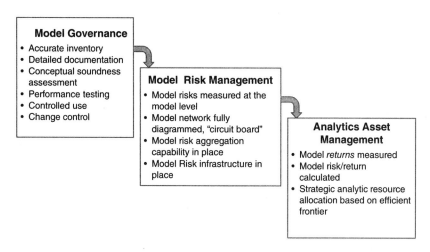

Figure 4.1 The Three Phases of Evolution in Model Management

across the evolutionary phases required to reach this goal, they need not be developed in a strictly sequential manner, but may be developed in parallel or overlapping intervals. For a firm pursuing such a long-term strategy for managing its model suite, it should be evident that the minimal requirements for model risk management insisted on by regulators would be insufficient and that the firm's own initiatives to govern and manage its model suite would far exceed any regulatory requirements or expectations. In this section we focus on the first two boxes in Figure 4.1. A discussion of evaluating the return, or productive capacity, of models is presented in Chapter 5.

MODEL GOVERNANCE

For an institution to effectively manage its analytic resources, which consist primarily of modelers and models, it needs to have a timely and comprehensive source of information about those resources. Most firms accomplish this through a model governance program of some kind; and indeed, model governance is a key focal point for most regulators. As a control function and a source of information for senior leadership, it is important that such a function be independent of the business analytic teams who develop and use the models. That way, much of the information that is produced *about* the models (which is inherently subjective) can at least be free from the bias that close association with the objectives of P&L might engender. As shown in Figure 4.1, some of the key functions that an independent model-governance group can perform are maintaining an accurate inventory of models currently in use, insuring that all such models are documented in an effective way, and performing independent assessments of model quality. Again, so much has been written about model governance at financial institutions that readers may be close to topic fatigue, and our objective here is not to discuss so-called best practices or regulatory expectations. Rather, we again look to view model governance as an information-creating process and a critical component of an institution's information management strategy.

We can begin by considering what information is being created and how its value can be maximized. In the first place, given the objective of managing the firm's information assets, the model inventory is itself information, and the associated metadata (data about the models) can be particularly high-value information. The effectiveness of the model governance will therefore be enhanced to the extent to which the inventory can be maintained in real-time, can contain the richest possible set of useful metadata, and can be digitized so that the information can flow through other information creating processes. Most large institutions forced into compliance with SR 11-7 or similar regulatory requirements have recognized that a model inventory cannot be effectively managed in a spreadsheet, and have sought to place the inventory process into a more capable technology. Many software vendors have begun to offer so-called model governance solutions, and comprehensive system offerings now usually include a model governance module of some sort to address this need. Many firms elect to build their own systems. But whatever the technological approach, its real value will not be in myopic servicing of the regulatory needs of the model governance group but in its ability to distribute information to related users and processes. For example, effective model risk measurement must depend on the completeness and accuracy of the inventory, as well as the availability of an array of model characteristics, performance, and risk measures being generated by the analysts who perform the independent validations. An effective process and system should standardize and digitize as much of this information as possible. Standardized measures of in-sample performance, parameter risk, operational risks, data quality risks, and other key observations of the model validators can all enrich a model risk measurement system—but not unless they are generated, expressed, and stored in a way that facilitates their use as quantitative inputs.

With an accurate model inventory embedded in an accessible database structure and an independent model validation process that produces, as a by-product of its governance and control function, granular, quantitative, multidimensional risk assessments, the construction of a structured quantitative model risk measurement framework and a strategic approach to resource allocation within the analytic layer are enabled.

DEFINING MODEL RISK

To manage models as the assets that they truly are, it is important to be able to view them both individually and as a portfolio in risk/return space. To associate risk measures with individual models as described in the prior section we need to have a working definition that we can apply. However, *model risk* is a term that lacks an accepted comprehensive industry-standard definition. Massimo Morini[1] provides a survey of the literature and identifies two classes of technical definitions of *model risk* currently in use. The first, the so-called *value approach* attributed to Derman, Morini summarizes as

> Model risk is the risk that the model is not a realistic/
> plausible representation of the factors affecting the
> derivative's (instrument's) *value*.

This definition focuses on conceptual soundness and the possibility that a model that we believe to be conceptually sound may in fact not be. Of the second, the so-called *price approach* attributed to Rebonato, Morini quotes

> Model risk is the risk of occurrence of a significant
> difference between the mark-to-model value of a complex
> and/or illiquid instrument, and the *price* at which the same
> instrument is revealed to have been traded in the market.

While the Federal Reserve definition of model risk under SR 11-7 is summarized as

> The use of models invariably presents model risk, which is the potential for adverse consequences from decisions based on incorrect or misused model outputs and reports. Model risk can lead to financial loss, poor business and strategic decision making, or damage to a bank's reputation. Model risk occurs primarily for two reasons:
>
> - The model may have fundamental errors and may produce inaccurate outputs when viewed against the design objective and intended business uses. The mathematical calculation and quantification exercise underlying any model generally involves application of theory, choice of sample design and numerical routines, selection of inputs and estimation, and implementation in information systems. Errors can occur at any point from design through implementation. In addition, shortcuts, simplifications, or approximations used to manage complicated problems could compromise the integrity and reliability of outputs from those calculations. Finally, the quality of model outputs depends on the quality of input data and assumptions, and errors in inputs or incorrect assumptions will lead to inaccurate outputs.
>
> - The model may be used incorrectly or inappropriately. Even a fundamentally sound model producing accurate outputs consistent with the design objective of the model may exhibit high model risk if it is misapplied or misused. Models by their nature are simplifications of reality, and real-world events may prove those simplifications inappropriate. This is even more of a concern if a model is used outside the environment for which it was designed. Banks may do this intentionally as

they apply existing models to new products or markets, or inadvertently as market conditions or customer behavior changes. Decision makers need to understand the limitations of a model to avoid using it in ways that are not consistent with the original intent. Limitations come in part from weaknesses in the model due to its various shortcomings, approximations, and uncertainties. Limitations are also a consequence of assumptions underlying a model that may restrict the scope to a limited set of specific circumstances and situations.[2]

This last definition focuses on a lack of concordance between the model output and the revealed factual evidence—an important type of measure, but one that may not apply well when the cause and effect linkage is not so straightforward, or when the time it takes to fully reveal the factual evidence is beyond the firm's risk tolerance horizon.

Evidently, the definitions referenced in Morini are directed primarily toward asset pricing models and the losses that a firm might experience as a result of using such models for investing and trading. And while the spirit of the two definitions could potentially be analogized, a definition useful for managing model risk across an entire institution must apply equally well to other classes of models. These should include reserving models, product pricing including insurance, consumer credit, and financial services, and various types of non-price forecasting models including stress-testing and economic capital, among others.

It seems that the *price approach* definition would be problematic to extend to all models for two reasons. In the first place, the broader category of models that we need to cover includes many for which no analogous *reality* is revealed. For example, a stress-testing model produces an if-this-scenario-then-that-outcome for relatively low probability scenarios. Thus, model risk is undefined until and unless the future unfolds in a way that is identical to one of the scenarios used as an input. And even then, the passage of time can render a test criterion invalid, since other things outside the model will have also changed by the time the result is in hand. For nonpricing models where an equivalent reality will be revealed, we could consider the relevant outcome to be equivalent to the reality of a price. In this way we would end up defining model risk to be the risk that any modeled quantity deviates from its expected (model-based) value. Some of the spirit of this ought to be included in a definition of model risk, but its strict application could be problematic depending on the context. Take for example, the case of a corporate probability of a default model. Such a model will always produce a number between zero and one, and the reality will always be either a zero or a one. In this case it makes sense to measure model risk at an aggregate level cross-sectionally or over time: in other words, does the *average* expected value differ from the *average* revealed outcome?

In most cases, use of the term *model risk* relates (at least in part) to the uncertainty borne by the model user as a result of the uncertainty embedded in the model. This embedded uncertainty is usually possible to describe or even precisely quantify statistically. Effectively, it is a known risk. In other cases, it includes both this known risk and the uncertainty borne by the user as a result of the possibility of model failure, of one or another sort. An effective model risk measurement framework must include the ability to assess models across the full spectrum of material failure modes, their heterogeneity notwithstanding.

OBJECTIFYING THE DOWNSIDE

It is well established in economic theory that the quantification of risk measures needs to be based on some explicit description of the preferences of the underlying economic agent who is faced with the risk. This principle applies equally well in the model risk context. That is, an institution will need to make some choices and express some preferences in order to have an effective, quantitative model risk measurement framework. It can do this by identifying and prioritizing the sorts of outcomes it wishes to avoid, the applicable time horizon, and how these bad outcomes rank in order of priority. By isolating and making explicit this subjective component of the framework, the institution can construct quantitative measurement and aggregation components on top of the risk model. Without this step, a true quantification of model risk is impossible.

Beyond the complexity introduced by the subjective aspect of risk, model risk quantification is complex because

- Risk at the model level is itself multidimensional.
- The various dimensions of model risk do not aggregate easily.
- Model's risks have term structure that may vary widely across multiple dimensions.
- Model risk can accumulate when models are used sequentially (that is, when model outputs are used as inputs into other models).
- Measurement of the exposure to the various model risks may require different treatment by model class and by risk type.

To overcome these complexities, we can organize the analysis around components of risk and classes of model characteristics, preserving different levels of granularity as necessary. A simple version of this component approach could be described with the following set of steps:

1. Identify a specific set of bad outcomes (risks) that the firm would like to avoid and associated time intervals, recognizing that some models generate risks with a term structure that may exceed that interval.

2. Organize the models into classes and identify the likelihood of occurrence during that interval for each of the bad outcomes should a model of that class fail or assumptions made based on the model turn out to be false, making adjustments where necessary to incorporate term structure effects.

3. For each model, calculate the likelihood that the model will fail or that assumptions made based on the model will turn out to be false.

4. For each model, calculate an exposure that measures the expected magnitude of each bad outcome should that bad outcome be manifest as a result of the model failing, or assumptions made based on the model turning out to be false.

5. Combine all of these elements. If a single model risk measure is desired, weigh the bad outcomes based on how much the firm would like to avoid each outcome and calculate a weighted average.

Risk Identification

In this simple framework, Steps 1 and 2 establish a relationship between a fixed set of risks and a fixed set of model classes. We can think of this as a model risk taxonomy that, while it may require some periodic review and evaluation for updating, is relatively static within any given institution. Such a taxonomy is illustrated with the hypothetical example in Figure 4.2. In this example, six model classes are associated with five risk types. The values in the grid are also intended to be illustrative with respect to the units of measurement, and dummies with respect to the values themselves. Potential value types include ordinal indexes or probabilities. In Figure 4.2, potential risk contribution can be thought of as the likelihood that an event of the designated risk type would occur if

Model Risk Taxonomy *Example*

Identified Risk Types

Model Class	Loss/ Unexpected Loss	Lost Revenue	Restatement of Financials	Other Reputational Impairment	Regulatory Risk
Asset Valuation	0.8	0.6	0.6	0.4	0.5
Credit Risk	0.9	0.8	0.4	0.4	0.5
Reserving	0.0	0.2	0.7	0.7	0.5
Loan Pricing	0.5	0.8	0.0	0.1	0.0
Hedging	0.3	0.5	0.2	0.3	0.4
Stress Testing	0.0	0.1	0.0	0.0	0.8

Contribution Potential

Figure 4.2 Hypothetical Model Risk Taxonomy

a model of that class experienced a failure. This is already a significant simplification, since as we discuss further below, models have different modes of failure that may yield different probabilities of bad outcomes.[3]

Such a taxonomy is important in that it helps to provide a granular view of what specific model risks are being borne by the firm, where that risk is coming from, and what strategies can be devised to reduce or remediate those risks. With this taxonomy in hand, we can flesh out the picture by combining it with model-specific data that indicates how likely the model is to fail (Step 3) and a measure of exposure to each model (Step 4).

As mentioned earlier, each type of model risk may have its own term structure. For example, a flawed insurance pricing model being used to underwrite policies at uneconomic rates may not have any near-term effect but may end up producing an income drag for many years into the future as claims rates run higher than expected for in-force policies. Similarly, a reserving model may underestimate reserves, requiring reserve additions that are an immediate drag on income, or it may overestimate reserves. In such a case, the release of reserves affects current income, but the maintenance of excess reserves over some prior interval would have acted as an income drag over that entire period. Alternatively, asset valuation models that turn out to be wrong are likely to produce write-offs at the time the error is identified, after which the model would likely be remediated or decommissioned. At some institutions and for some purposes, Step 1 can restrict the risk measure to focus solely on loss, either over a 12-month period (generally in an ECAP context) or over nine quarters (in a CCAR context). But to place model risk measurement on a common basis for all models it will be necessary to use a common time interval over which downside effects can be measured.

Evaluating how likely the model is to fail and what modes of failure comprise that overall likelihood requires detailed model-by-model analysis. The corporate function best positioned to apply a consistent and unbiased analysis of this type is the independent model validation function, which should already be performing this analysis and managing the model inventory for the firm. The goal, then, is to harvest enough information from the ongoing validation process to feed the model risk measurement process. This may entail some tweaking to the validation process itself to ensure that the required outputs are being generated. These required outputs will support assessments of the underlying model failure drivers, which include

- Data challenges, risks, and deficiencies
- Methodology and assumption risks (including model specification error)
- Statistical performance failure (outlier occurrence risks)
- Implementation and usage risks

Of these, many will need to cast in ways that are appropriate for a particular model class. For example, statistical performance measures may be easier to define and far more relevant for asset valuation models and reserving models than for stress-testing models. For the former, the question needs to be framed in terms of expected deviance versus unexpected deviance—in other words, what level of imprecision did the model users accept when the model was deployed and what level of imprecision would be considered a model failure? Different statistical measures will likely need to be selected for various types of models. To implement such an approach, inherent uncertainty measures need to be harvested from the model validation process. While quantities like precision and parameter uncertainty, which could be measurable, model specification error is not measurable and will have to be assessed subjectively. However, the model development process ought to be extremely sensitive to model specification error risk and should provide strong supporting evidence in support of the proposed specification relative to alternatives, as shown in Figure 4.3. Accordingly, the assessment performed by the model validation group can be centered around the extent to which specification error risk has already been assessed and mitigated. Since the first-order goal of the framework is the rank ordering of models by model risk, rank orderings of these risk components are sufficient to make the framework operational as long as they are consistently applied.

From the previous bullet points it can be observed that many of the underlying causes of model failure are of the operational variety, as opposed the statistical variety. Operational risks are notoriously hard to assess *ex ante*, but some subjective assessment of these same issues

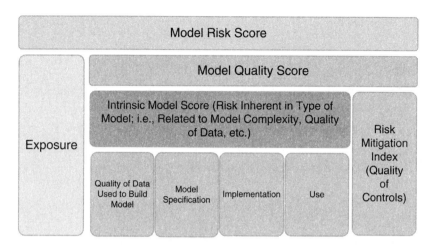

Figure 4.3 Components of a Model Risk Measure

must already exist if the firm is performing adequate model validations. Again, the goal is to standardize these assessments as much as possible (at least within model classes) and fit them into a rank ordering scheme that is consistent with the real perceived likelihood of model failure for that model class.

There are certainly a variety of ways of approaching this. Satyam Kancharla of Numerix[4] provides some suggestions and a case study that presents an approach to collecting operational and performance risks on a model-by-model basis. To complete Step 3, we need to combine the operational and inherent statistical risk measures. This will necessarily be somewhat ad hoc, but to deploy a working model risk measurement framework it is not necessary to develop a technique that is supported by theory or can lay any claim to being optimal. The rank ordering of models must be done in a way that constituents agree makes sense.

We may need to add another category of risk that reflects the potential for risks to be propagated and cumulated as model outputs are used both directly and as inputs into other models. This may be more relevant for complex institutions in which processes like stress testing create sequential model dependencies. For lack of a better term we call this *model nesting*, and it creates a situation in which a model failure may have both direct effects and indirect effects since the model's outputs served as inputs into another downstream process.

Residual Error   **Outputs Used as Inputs to Other Models**

Model	Inherent Uncertainty	Op Risk Score	Nesting Penalty	Final Inherent Model Risk Measure
Reserving 2	0.13	0.05	1	0.18
Reserving 1	0.2	0.05	1	0.25
PD 1	0.22	0.25	1	0.47
Reserving 3	0.45	0.05	1	0.50
PD2	0.29	0.25	1	0.54
LGD 1	0.35	0.2	1	0.55
Interest Rate Hedging 1	0.15	0.4	1.2	0.66
Asset Valuation 2	0.53	0.2	1.2	0.88
Asset Valuation 3	0.23	0.4	1.4	0.88
Asset Valuation 1	0.67	0.3	1.2	1.16

Model Risk Measures Captured Through
the Independent Validation Process   *All Other Operational Risks*

Figure 4.4 Hypothetical Model Risk Assessments

One simple approach is to penalize (raise the risk measure) of models that have significant and/or multilayered downstream dependencies. To illustrate a simple application of Step 3, Figure 4.4 presents a hypothetical list of models scored by component and ranked lowest to highest in terms of risk.

In Steps 3 and 4, we attempt to summarize the relationship between the likelihood that a modeled value will have error and the cost associated with that error. We have already simplified the problem substantially by restricting our attention to costs associated with a specific, discrete set of outcomes. We can simplify it even further. Given a probabilistic characterization of the error potential, we could try to integrate the cost function over the whole probability range to obtain an expected cost. However, we are primarily interested in the downside and because we need to acknowledge the possibility that any model will have been incorrectly defined or that environmental changes have rendered the model obsolete, it does not make sense to overinvest in an approach that treats an empirical error distribution as a forward probability distribution. Finally, since (as already discussed) our model risk measurement framework needs to be founded on an expression of preferences, we can express those preferences through the selection of a model error-cost linkage that is also practical from an implementation perspective.

After having considered the details of risk and exposure measurement at the model level, let's consider how the pieces fit together from an infrastructure and information flow perspective. To make such a framework effective *as a process*, it needs to be implementable as an automated or semiautomated reporting system. It cannot be overemphasized that to effectively manage a complex suite of models, the model risk measurement framework needs to yield a *current* view of model risk covering all models in use and reportable in a simple and transparent way.

In this approach, the required input data can be grouped together naturally by both type and frequency. The taxonomy itself is a key input, and while it may require periodic updating or tweaking, it can be viewed as effectively static. Model risk measures need to be harvested from the model validation and review process. That is, multiple measurements of each models' statistical and operational vulnerabilities are the key foundational elements of any model risk measurement system, and these need to obtained from the independent model review and ongoing monitoring processes. Given industry best practices and regulatory guidance requiring annual review, this would create at a minimum a continual flow of annual observation data into the model risk measurement system coming from the independent validation process. However, to the extent that ongoing model performance monitoring processes are in place, as should be the case for models generating higher-frequency flows of actual versus predicted outcomes, these higher-frequency performance statistics should also be flowing into the system as inputs. Exposure data is the third key input, and this can be flowed into the system at any frequency depending on availability, although high-frequency or real-time data linkages improve the timeliness and quality of the desired reporting. These three input data classes are presented on the left side of Figure 4.5.

As described above, Step 3 requires the production of multiple measurements of each model's statistical and operational vulnerabilities, and this requires a detailed examination of the performance characteristics and failure modes of each individual model. This

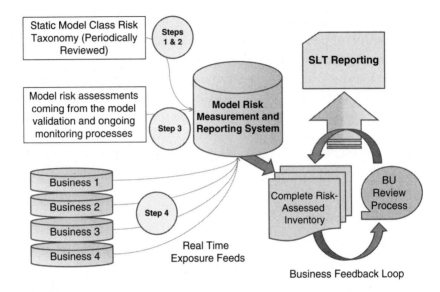

Figure 4.5 Schematic Diagram of a Model Risk Reporting System

analysis needs to include measures of at least three components of model performance including

1. Expected uncertainty (which includes in-sample error characteristics such as residual squared error, or appropriate statistical confidence intervals, etc.) and parameter error (which is the additional uncertainty surrounding estimated parameters where such parameters exist).

2. Potential uncertainty (which includes both gross specification error, or the extent to which the developed model is wrong relative to the historical data on which it was based, and obsolescence, or the potential for the model to underperform due to changes in the environment, changes in the behavior of relevant agents, or both).

3. Operational risk per se (which is the potential for the model to fail due to process or other operational breakdowns, or for the model to be used inappropriately producing model user error).

To operationalize expected uncertainty as a risk measure, we need to select a specific function of the family of available statistics to base the measure on, and this will vary from model to model based on model specification and the context in which the model is being used. For example, for a regression model we may choose any number of statistics derived from the distribution of residuals, such as variance, semivariance, two standard deviations, an arbitrary high quantile like 99.9 percent, a quantile tied to exogenously given stress level, and so on. Potential uncertainty stemming from unperceived model specification error can only be partially assessed, but model validators may still be able to form an opinion and score this risk level based on elements they observe during their validations. These may include aspects of the dynamics of the phenomenon being modeled, such as the extent to which the risk level is driven by technology, human psychology, or fragile supply/demand relationships. Or the elements may include model-specific features, such as the strength of the underlying theory, the depth or quality of the data used to fit the model, and the robustness of the modeling technique.

As a whole, Step 3 may sound like an enormous task, especially for a firm that has many hundreds or even several thousands of models deployed. However, this perception seems to be unique to the financial services industry. In other industries that rely heavily on quantitative models to drive performance and even protect the existence of the firm—such as aerospace, pharmaceuticals, and structural engineering—understanding model performance ranges, failure modes, and limitations are simply standard business practice. For banks and other regulated financial service providers, these diagnostic requirements are now being required by regulators. Properly instituted, detailed model validation work (that, after all, is required anyway) can be oriented toward supporting a variety of adjacent uses by the firm, including a consistent model risk-measurement framework. Ensuring that detailed model validations do produce, as a byproduct, those statistical measures required to support a prespecified model risk measurement framework is one of the main tasks of a financial institution seeking to gain a competitive advantage through superior information management. Taken together, the joint requirements that all models receive thorough independent validation and that model performance must be reviewed at least annually, can help a firm establish a process by which the inputs required in Step 3 are flowing at an annual rate with little ongoing marginal cost.

Model Risk Exposure

Step 4 is perhaps the most challenging aspect of the framework construction, and many subtleties exist. The goal of this component is to assess the magnitude of each potential bad outcome conditional on the model's failure. But deciding what quantity to use to assess magnitude is not trivial. In the first place, no universal basis exists. Certain classes of models affect *stock* values (such as reserves, asset values, and capital) while other classes affect *flow* values (such as current and future income, sales volume, and various cash flows). Even within these classes different bases may be required. For example, an appropriate basis for the weighting of models used to value assets like bonds and loans might be the face value of exposure, whereas an appropriate basis for derivatives models might be potential future exposure (PFE). In the second place, a term structure of individual risks may also exist, forcing us to either select a time interval as a common basis or live with exposure measures that are not fully consistent. To illustrate, consider a model whose failure might lead to a string of losses over a string of successive years versus a model whose failure might produce only one loss that would be immediately recognized. An obvious solution would be to put all losses on a one-year basis and simply discount expected future losses back to the current year. But even this obvious solution may have subtleties as the risk of model failure is not merely the risk that the model will fail, but rather the risk that it will have failed during some time interval that includes both past and future time. Moreover, consider the first two columns of the chart in Figure 4.2, which relate separately to impacts on the balance sheet and income statement. Under some strong assumptions one could convert everything into an asset basis or an income basis. For example, one could put everything on an income basis simply by multiplying balance sheet losses by return on assets (ROA). Alternatively, one could view the two types of losses differently and, since both are in dollar terms, weight them according to some preference. For example, a firm might choose to measure each as proportional effects, dividing lost income by net income and lost asset value by total assets.

Exposure definition may be approached at the model class level or may require additional granularity depending in part on the complexity of the institution and its product array. Clearly, a risk exposure measure will need to relate specific models to the bad outcomes enumerated in Step 1. Obviously, the exposure measure will be probabilistic in nature, since we cannot specify precisely what failure mode will be manifest, nor what the environmental conditions will be or what other risk mitigants might be in place at the time. Let's consider an example of one particular model, and see what challenges arise as we try to define exposure to the multiple outcome types listed in Figure 4.2.

First let's consider an asset valuation model used for an illiquid asset class for which secondary market prices are unavailable. Such a model has the potential to produce a wide range of bad outcomes (all of them in Figure 4.2) under a scenario in which the underlying asset experiences significant loss of value, including reduced dividend income. From a *loss* perspective, exposure could clearly be tied directly to the size of the firm's position for that asset class.[5] Given that both the expected uncertainty and potential uncertainty determined in Step 3 are likely to be expressed as probability distributions of loss in percentage terms, using a dollar-based exposure measure seems to make sense. But it still remains to be determined what basis should apply for the other risks that this model is exposing the firm to. The next three risk categories in our example are *restatement of financials, other reputational impairment,* and *regulatory risk.* Strong consideration might be given to viewing these as binary outcome modes. That is, rather than trying to evaluate the impact of these outcomes on a continuum, weighted by exposure or otherwise, one could simply develop an average expected cost associated with each of these outcomes. This simplifies the analysis considerably and in certain cases could simplify the likelihood measure also, reducing it to the identification of a materiality threshold beyond which we would presume the event to be triggered.

Consider specifically the restatement of financials category. It would seem noncontroversial that if model failure could require a firm to formally restate its financial disclosures this risk type should be broken out as a specific category of model risk. As an informed observer wrote, "Restatements can be drawn out and expensive processes and may require management to communicate with many different stakeholders including the Board of Directors, auditors, regulators and shareholders...."[6] A study of over 12,000 financial restatements[7] found that the most common issues that resulted in restatements in 2012 and the rates of their occurrence were

1. Improper measurement of debt, stock warrants, and equity (15 percent).

2. Tax expense/benefit/deferral and other FAS 109 issues (14.6 percent).

3. Cash flow statement classification errors (13.3 percent).

4. Acquisitions, mergers, and reorganization accounting issues (12.1 percent).

5. Revenue recognition issues (9.5 percent).

6. Accounts/loans receivable, investments, and cash valuation issues (8.7 percent).

7. Liabilities, payables, reserves, and accrual estimate failures (8.3 percent).

Items 1, 6, and 7 are activities heavily dependent on models, while 2 and 5 frequently involve model-based forecasts and estimates. Without details about the causes of individual problems we can only speculate as to how directly model failures played a role; however, for many of the largest and highest profile restatements model failure is known to have been a key cause. One high profile example that is instructive is the so-called London Whale case described in Chapter 9.

Securities and Exchange Commission (SEC) guidelines require that adjustments to financial statement data be material if published financials are to be restated. Thus, if the institution would not expect to restate financials for an asset revaluation below $500 million, then the restatement of financials risk for an asset valuation model should be based on the probability that the model error would exceed $500 million. Following the binary outcome approach suggested earlier, the institution would also have to come up with an estimate of the expected or average cost of restating financials. Multiplying that by the probability that the model error exceeds the threshold produces a risk measure *for this specific risk, for this specific model.*

Other reputational impairment is also an important risk category for financial institutions precisely because the market is so competitive and depositors, customers, and other financial counterparties are skittish when it comes to reputational threats or damage. Of course, this risk reflects the product line, market, and commercial climate in which the activity is taking place, so the measurement of risk exposure will need to include some subjective assessment of these factors that can be taken down to the model level. In practice, it may be most effective to apply reputational risk exposure factors by model class or LOB (line of business), as opposed to making separate assessments at the individual model level.

The simple fact, revealed through the sequence of highly publicized model failures, is that model-related losses can be of different types and can manifest themselves in different ways. There may not be a single methodologically pure way of footing such loss events onto a common basis, nor is it necessarily appropriate to elevate methodological purity over practicality. The top 10 riskiest models within any firm could probably be equally well identified by any number of exposure measurement schemes, as well as by expert judgment. Moreover, for large institutions the same could probably be said for major business lines. For this reason, and because to lever a model risk measurement system to its widest range of uses requires significant buy-in from multiple constituents, it makes sense to tune the system using a subjective assessment process. As depicted in the lower right quadrant of Figure 4.5, a risk-ranked model inventory is one of the key outputs of the framework. This list can be reviewed by the senior leadership team (SLT) and business unit (BU) lists can be reviewed by business level leaders to provide a smell test. Models that appear well out of place are signals that either the taxonomy or the exposure measure is not effectively calibrated, or that the model-specific risk features have not been effectively captured. Since the framework can be largely automated, tweaks to address smell-test failures are cheap and iterative improvements can quickly build credibility and usefulness.

MODEL RISK ATTRIBUTION: AN INFORMATION ENTROPY APPROACH

One benefit of taking an information-centric view of financial institutions' core functions is that in certain instances some aspects of information theory[8] (largely due to Claude Shannon[9]) can be levered, either explicitly or in spirit. Model risk assessment and attribution is one case in which certain aspects of the theory may be applied in useful ways. In order to do this we have to make the leap to viewing model outputs as signals in the presence of noise and actual outcomes as the truth embedded in those signals. In other words, we need to think of the modeled quantity—say, the future empirical volatility of some traded asset—as a message emanating from an ergodic source[10] and the actual model output as a signal in which that message may be more or less efficiently embedded and may also be contaminated by some noise. These are certainly heroic assumptions, particularly the assumption of ergodicity, since the world is always changing and the causes of modeled phenomena are never stable. However, if we allow ourselves to fit the somewhat square peg of financial modeling into the round hole of information theory we can take a somewhat different view of model risk and in some cases adopt helpful quantitative methods to assess that risk.

In particular, a fallacy that we will wish to avoid is the confounding of *model risk* with *risk that exists*, just because a model is present. To avoid this problem, it may be useful to view models as devices that inform by reducing uncertainty. For example, suppose we require forward volatility estimates for two currencies; say, the Japanese yen (JPY) and the euro (EUR). In the absence of a model to forecast what the volatilities would be we might simply use historical averages. These are presented in Table 4.1. From the table we can see that the volatility of the JPY is higher than that of the EUR, but the volatility of the volatility is also higher. In fact, the maximum volatility as a proportion of average volatility is also higher for the JPY. In information theory terms we would say the *uncertainty* surrounding the forward volatility is higher or that the *entropy* of the JPY estimate is higher, since its volatility is more volatile.

Now suppose we could employ two separate prediction models for each, each of which is capable of producing forecasts accurate to within 5 percent of realized volatility. This will significantly reduce the entropy in both cases, as well as equating the entropy across the two. How should we view these two models from a model risk perspective? Certainly the model for the JPY would do more work (since it

Table 4.1 Daily Return Volatility Measures

	JPY	EUR
Avg. Mo. Vol.	6.43%	4.97%
Max Vol.	30.44%	22.08%
Vol. of Vol.	8.64%	7.47%

would have to eliminate more uncertainty to reach the 5 percent target) and that should be recognized in a model risk measure. Another important observation is that from an entropy perspective, *both models are reducing uncertainty, not adding to it,* and so do not appear to be adding any risk. It's true that the models could be wrong, but the likelihood for error seems to be higher without the services of the models than after their introduction. The data in Table 4.1 were obtained from the V-Lab website[11] at New York University, created by the Volatility Institute under the direction of Professor Robert Engle which also provides a variety of models designed to forecast volatility and a variety of performance measures to evaluate them.

To make this more concrete with another example, consider a situation in which an institution needs to measure the risk in two corporate portfolios, each containing 200 individual credit exposures. Suppose further that one is a high-grade portfolio drawn from a population whose long-term average default rate was 2 percent and one is a spec-grade portfolio drawn from a population whose average long-term default rate is 10 percent, and that we use two separate models to estimate individual PDs for the exposures in the two portfolios. Intuitively, it is easy to see how much lower the entropy is in the high-grade portfolio. One can think of it this way: How many defaulters do we need to identify to resolve the uncertainty in each portfolio? For the high-grade portfolio it is four. Once those four defaulters are identified we know that the rest of the individuals in the portfolio will not default. In contrast, for the spec-grade portfolio we need to identify 20 defaulters—*five times in the number required for the high-grade portfolio*—to know conclusively who will and who will not default, and thus eliminate the uncertainty in the portfolio. Following Pierce,[12] we can calculate the entropy directly using the formula

$$H_h = -\sum_{200} 0.02 \times \log(0.02) = 22.58$$

for the high-grade portfolio and

$$H_s = -\sum_{200} 0.10 \times \log(0.10) = 66.44$$

for the spec-grade portfolio.

In this calculation, h is the entropy measure and log is the logarithm of base 2. We will not try to derive or fully explain this formula here, except to point out that for binary outcome, the function is symmetric, reaching a maximum at 0.5—the point where uncertainty is highest. The explanation provided by Pierce is highly recommended for interested readers. Returning to our example, we can see that there's more uncertainty in the spec-grade portfolio; an intuitive result, since *in the case of the high-grade portfolio we already know most of the obligors will not default*. With these pools of obligors so characterized we can ask what will happen when we introduce a model. Again, we should extend our intuition a bit as a first step, prior to any evaluation of the statistical models. To explore this question, first consider the entropy of these two portfolios combined. This is a portfolio of 400 names with an average expected default rate of 24/400 = 6 percent and a combined entropy measure of

$$H_C = -\sum_{400} 0.06 \times \log(0.06) = 97.41$$

That number, 97.41, is 9.4 percent higher than the sum of the two subportfolio entropy measures of 89.01 (66.44 + 22.58). The reason for this is that in the first case we have the additional information that allowed us to construct the two subportfolios and characterize them statistically. In other words, *we already had, and were using, a model*—the model that separated high-grade from spec-grade. And that model was measurably reducing our uncertainty, which means reducing our risk.

The generalization to more refined credit models is straightforward. Any additional model (or combinations of models) that we can bring to bear to further segment this portfolio—by likelihood of default, EDFs, or refined credit ratings, for example—may reduce entropy, which can be viewed as reducing overall risk. This entropy reduction can be easily measured, heroic assumptions notwithstanding. Likewise, any volatility model that reduces forward estimation error reduces entropy and reduces overall risk.

The cost-benefit analysis associated with a choice between models, or the choice about whether to spend resources to improve a model, can thus be clearly represented as the cost of a marginal reduction in entropy versus the benefit of a marginal reduction in entropy. Importantly, this means the analysis for any given model must use as its basis the entropy that would have existed prior to the introduction of the model in question. That is, the model's contribution cannot be effectively measured unless we have a measure of the entropy that existed before the model was introduced. This challenges the institution to try to consider the entropy it faces in each critical ongoing business decision-making activity. In many cases the problem will not lend itself to such a characterization, either because the activity itself is too unstructured (such as discretionary opportunistic hedging, or proprietary trading), or because the process being modeled stretches the assumptions of information so far as to distort an approximate entropy measure. But in cases in which the entropy level can be evaluated, a performance criterion that can be used across model types and use classes is established. This is the conditional information entropy ratio or CIER.[13]

Under this view, a model that does not increase CIER should not be used not matter what its cost, and a model that does increase CIER is reducing risk. What about the model risk? The fact that a measure like CIER indicates a reduction in risk doesn't prove that risk has been reduced. It is, after all, a statistical measure based on historical data and some assumptions that are anywhere from unlikely to impossible to hold. The world may change and the model may suddenly become wrong or perform poorly. Or the data underlying the model and the statistics may turn out to have been wrong. And, as always, even if the model and measurement are correct the model could be used out of context or otherwise misused causing loss to the institution. The point is that an effective overall information management framework includes features that minimize or control these risks too, so that the more advanced the institution is in these other related areas, the higher will be the applicability of entropy-based measures to evaluate the risk/return contribution of models.

NOTES

1. Massimo Morini, *Understanding and Managing Model Risk: A Practical Guide for Quants, Traders and Validators* (Chichester, UK: John Wiley & Sons, 2011), 4–7.

2. Board of Governors, Federal Reserve, "SR 11-7," April 4, 2011, 3, www.federal reserve.gov/bankinforeg/srletters/sr1107a1.pdf.

3. The additional dimension of variability in modes of failure could be included in the framework if the institution had enough information to parse the separate modes of failure by likelihood and severity for each model.

4. Satyam Kancharla, "Mastering Model Risk: Assessment, Regulation and Best Practices," Numerix Research (October 2013).

5. This relationship facilitates automation, as will be discussed in the section entitled "Model Risk Attribution: An Information Entropy Approach."

6. Chad Kokenge, "Restatements," PricewaterhouseCoopers, accessed October 8, 2014, www.pwc.com/us/en/audit-assurance-services/accounting-advisory/restatements .jhtml.

7. Audit Analytics used data from over 7,000 SEC public registrants between 2001 and 2012.

8. Alternately, communication theory.

9. See, for example, Claude Shannon and Warren Weaver, *The Mathematical Theory of Communication* (Urbana: University of Illinois Press, 1949).

10. An ergodic source is effectively a source that doesn't change—false in this case.

11. NYU Volatility Institute, http://vlab.stern.nyu.edu/analysis.

12. John R. Pierce, *An Introduction to Information Theory: Symbols, Signals and Noise* (New York: Dover Publications, 1980).

13. For a detailed discussion of CIER, see Jorge R. Sobehart, Sean C. Keenan, and Roger Stein, "Complexities and Validation of Default Risk Models," in *Frontiers in Credit Risk*, ed. Gordian Gaeta (Hoboken, NJ: John Wiley & Sons, 2003), 179–211.

CHAPTER **5**

The Return on
Analytic Assets

conomists have long used the concept of a production function to organize thinking about and abstractly represent how multiple inputs are converted into output. In introductory economics courses (and beyond), the concept is often cast in terms of two primary inputs, labor and capital. This may constitute an oversimplification in many contexts but is potentially relevant in ours, particularly when we recognize that a financial institution's capital (in the economic sense, not the financial sense) consists largely of its information processing system.

At its core, the fundamental use of production functions is cost-benefit analysis under feasibility constraints and the identification of an optimal mix of inputs. The actual estimation of production functions has a somewhat checkered history and has seen some of its most successful applications at the industrial or sector level for broader economic planning and policy purposes. At the firm level, actually estimating functional relationships is meaningful only when processes and technologies are stable over time and the data needed to estimate the functions is available. Neither of these two conditions applies over most of the range of products and services offered by financial institutions. And yet the revenue generated through the provision of these products and services is effectively the result of combining labor and capital, where the capital is the relevant component of the firm's information processing complex. Obviously, each firm has an internal process by which it decides who, and how many, to hire, and how much it will pay these hires. In many cases these human resource management processes are sophisticated and tied to a variety of performance measures specific to each business line. But if the firm neglects to pay a similar amount of attention to its plant and equipment, then the potential material performance gains from a more strategic investment in, and deployment of, plant and equipment will be left on the table. Furthermore, the rate at which a financial institution can convert data into information is among the most fundamental features of its production function and, importantly, *this key feature is, or should be, largely under its own control.* In this chapter we discuss how a financial institution can approach better, more informed cost-benefit analysis of the inputs into its production processes, even if these fall short of the estimation of economic production functions.

MEASURING THE PRODUCTIVITY OF MODELS

The practical difficulties associated with specifying an actual analytic production function for a financial institution or its component businesses center around problems with units of measurement and with output attribution. These problems also carry through to efforts to perform less technical, but still valuable, cost-benefit analyses. Therefore, an institution should ask itself what aspects of its process structure make these problems worse or better and seek to evolve processes to support more effective future analyses.

Typically economists like to view productivity in terms of physical units of capital, such as machine hours, applied over a fixed time horizon. A natural analogue for financial institutions might be something like *model months*. However, models can be replicated and distributed in ways that machines cannot, and so the concept might need to be refined to something like *man model months* to reflect the fact that many people could be using the same model at the same time. But this is still not satisfactory, since models seldom run over extended time intervals like machines but instead yield results either immediately or after short bursts of computational exertion. As a practical matter, it is of primary interest to understand how improving model performance can improve business performance and of lesser importance to understand whether models can be substituted for labor (or vice versa) while maintaining a given level of business volume. Therefore it may be more productive to focus on understanding the productive characteristics of each inventoried model *as used*.

The allocation challenges stem from two sources. First (as noted above), many people could be using the same model, which would be counted as one model in the inventory, or many people could be using essentially the same model separately, with each instance counted as an individual model in the inventory. While this is perfectly fine (if costly from a model governance perspective), it can weaken the linkage between the models and their performance measurements. For example, suppose that a coin (which may or may not be fair) is being flipped repeatedly. If we use a single model to estimate the likelihood of heads we can quickly gauge over successive flips the accuracy of the model as well as the entropy reduction over the naïve assumption that the coin is fair. But if we use a different model for each flip we won't accumulate any such information. Therefore, if too many separate model instances are allowed to operate simultaneously, or if model versions are released too rapidly, the contribution of individual models to financial performance will be that much harder to assess. Secondly, most processes involve complex blends of human judgment and the outputs from (possibly) multiple models. In such cases, any one model's contribution to the revenue from a product or service may be too indirect to isolate quantitatively. But again, all that is really required is some answer to the question of how business performance would be affected if the model's performance were significantly better or significantly worse.

To structure the problem better and align it with the model risk measurement framework described in Chapter 4 we could begin by making the following determinations for each model:

- Is the model fulfilling a pure compliance role?
- If the model is not just fulfilling a compliance role, is there a positive association between model performance and business/transaction profitability?

● Is there a term-structure of return, such that an improvement or deterioration of model performance will affect current and future profitability?

For models that are successfully fulfilling pure compliance functions (say, for example, mandatory regulatory stress testing models or even economic capital models), the productive contribution has already reached a maximum. Such models are required for the business to operate. Great care, however, should be given to the identification of models that are simply required to do business and serve no other productive capacity. First it should be asked, "Is it impossible that a so-identified model could have some marginal impact on income? Or is it just the way we've chosen to use it?" That is, could it be a red flag for price-taking behavior or other behavior that frustrates the maximal use of available information? Or, in the case of economic capital models, is there no productive use of the output other than compliance? Could the model not contribute to a more efficient allocation of capital, one that we could measure? Second, even if the model truly is a process requirement with no marginal effect on performance (a pure regulatory requirement, for example) then it should be subjected to the highest level of control, since income truly depends on it. In terms of our model risk taxonomy presented in Figure 4.3, such models should be given very high coefficients for the risks that apply—regulatory risk, reputational risk, and restatement of financials—and managed accordingly.

For models that are direct contributors to the generation of income, the nature of that contribution requires some characterization before its financial impact can be assessed. Models typically contribute either through helping to increase volume, helping to improve profitability, or both. For example, in consumer credit businesses models typically establish acceptance and credit limit criteria simultaneously, factors which drive acquisition rates and expected loss/expected return rates. These businesses are generally very advanced in terms of their ability to associate incremental model-performance gains with business performance metrics. This is reflected in their levels of investment in model innovation and criteria for the adoption of newer models. But the ability of consumer credit businesses to make such quantitative associations is by no means accidental. It is enabled by an overall business model that has information processing as a core competency. The careful accumulation and quantitative assessment of delinquency rates, card usage, applications, and lapses are core functions of the business. More importantly, the use of specific models is carefully tracked so that the connection between model-based decisions and outcomes can be made easily and electronically. With these information flows in place the quantitative assessment of the economic contribution of a model, and incremental improvements to a model, become straightforward.

Certain models contribute to financial performance through risk mitigation and the stabilization of earnings, as opposed to volume or current profitability. Reserving models, for example, estimate embedded loss that was generated through the use of multiple models over time as the reserved-for portfolio was built. So while individual losses that materialize should be associated with their *ex post* risk models (whatever they are), the movement of reserves over time represents performance volatility at the firm level that ought to be minimized. Since the *expected value* of losses is tied to other models, it is the *unexpected value* of losses that reserving models serve to manage. Adverse reserve developments cannot be avoided, but if they can be identified early they can be smoothed somewhat. Of course, reserve volatility that stems from model revisions (as opposed to changes in loss patterns) represents unnecessary volatility that management would like to avoid.

For many model classes, particularly pricing models for long-term asset or liability positions, economic contribution measurement is complicated by the term structure associated with return accumulation and recognition. Consider commercial loan underwriting in most institutions. Each asset only pays off over time, and future events with enormous impact on the total return (such as defaults) need to be known with certainty before empirical returns can be calculated. Obviously the transaction returns, and therefore model returns, need to be measured over time. This requires the institution to be able to identify at any time during the life of a loan which models were used to underwrite and price the transaction and the ability to calculate a final empirical return when the transaction concludes, including empirical all-in recoveries for defaulted transactions. For many institutions such a capability does not exist. In fact, many institutions utilize hurdle rates based on criteria like ROE (return on equity) or ROI (return on investment) to approve transactions and even measure business line performance. But these are *prospective* ROE or ROI values that rely on forecasts, typically produced by models, not values that reflect actual returns. For an institution to have an automated *model performance* capability for commercial transactions, it needs to have an automated *transaction performance* monitoring capability. That is, for every transaction it needs to be able calculate and plot the expected ROE (or other metric) at the time of underwriting versus the actual ROE received when the transaction is terminated, and it needs to be able to associate each transaction with the models that were used to approve, price, and structure the deal.

A similar argument may be made for insurance pricing. For insurance products, differentiation may be made based on transaction size, with consumer insurance products getting more of a cohort treatment, as is done in the consumer credit businesses. Again, the key is to have an accurate model inventory containing all of the relevant metadata, and to make sure that all policies underwritten are associated electronically with the models that were used to acquire, structure, and price the exposure.

COMPLEMENTARITY OF DATA INFLOW
WITH INFORMATION PROCESSING

A production function view of the financial institution, even if simplistic, affords some immediate insights with respect to the management of the information flows that are critical to the firm's success. An analogy with manufacturing firms helps to reinforce one of these key insights: *The flow of raw data into the firm needs to be balanced against the capacity of the firm to process that input into usable outputs.* Simply put, an efficient institution ought to know how much raw data it is accumulating through operations and data purchases, and it should believe that that quantity is effectively balanced against its data processing capabilities and the productivity gains that could be obtained through acquiring and processing more data.[1] Not enough data means limited information creation, which could mean less than optimally informed decision making. Too much data is unlikely to be a direct cost problem, given the low cost of storage. However, when data is acquired or even accumulated internally but not effectively distributed out into the various analytic and reporting activity centers, or if the data is accumulated in ways that frustrate the application of effective data quality controls, then the ratio of data accumulated to usable processed outputs will be low. Moreover, haphazard accumulation of data may be adding complexity to the system design and absorbing critical IT resources to manage. Finally, the accumulation of data needs to be balanced against the ability to control data quality. Beyond the operational risks that arise from inadequate data quality control, poor data quality is an efficiency drag on information conversion. Estimates are that between 50 and 80 percent of the time that modelers spend devoted to building a model is spent on data cleaning and data preparation. To improve competitive performance it is therefore necessary to target the dual goals of providing modelers with more data and reducing the time they need to spend cleaning and checking it.

Obviously a firm cannot measure its accumulation of data if it is not accumulating data in a controlled way. When the firm allows for a multiplicity of data entry and internal data accumulation points, it can complicate the process of monitoring data accumulation to the point of infeasibility. As discussed earlier, when external data is being acquired by multiple constituencies for their own specific local uses and stored in local data marts, the institution will not be able to effectively monitor the accumulation itself, much less associate the data with the uses for which it has been acquired. This applies equally to internally generated data. To reemphasize a point made earlier, without the ability to catalogue acquired/generated data and associate it with its uses, the firm is exposed to redundant data accumulation, which would distort any calculation of the conversion of data into information. Redundant data (and service) acquisition is so widespread in the financial services industry that Dun & Bradstreet created a service to identify possible redundancies by scrubbing vendor contract data and billing records to identify duplicative contracts. Likewise, the firm should have some capability to measure the flow and accumulation of model outputs. To measure both raw data accumulation and the flow of outputs in an automated and structured way, it is essential for the infrastructure to differentiate exhaustively between the two. This means either flagging all data elements with indicators, or, more efficiently, creating separate storage repositories—one for raw data, and a separate one for model outputs. This is discussed further in Chapter 7.

A DIGRESSION ON PRICE TAKING

It should be fairly obvious that the goal of greater capacity for production of information is more informed decision making. But while more informed decision making is viewed as critical to competitive advantage in many of the activities undertaken by financial institutions, in some institutions and for some activities it is not. These are typically those in which compensation and performance are tied primarily to volume targets, and may include certain types of underwriting, such as syndicated loans and (at least pre-crisis) mortgage-backed securities of various kinds. They may also include asset purchases and various kinds of hedging. The hallmark of activities in which more information is not viewed as helpful is that the participants identify themselves as *price takers*.[2] There is an extreme form of the efficient-market hypothesis that holds that for traded assets all of the information relevant to the valuation of those assets is embedded in the current price. However, while this idea is interesting as an intellectual curiosity, it doesn't match the empirical evidence in most cases. The history of asset prices is rife with cases in which very large price changes demonstrated that prior prices were, in some sense, misinformed. Moreover, even to the extent that market prices are informed, the mechanism for infusing prices with information must be the continued appearance of traders who are marginally better informed and who communicate that information to other traders through trades that move prices. Rebonato elegantly explains that "Ultimately, whenever a trader enters a position, he must believe that, in some sense, the market is 'wrong.'"[3] We can modify this sensibly by saying that whenever traders choose, or are forced, to make trades, they should seek to be as informed as possible given the constraints, and hope that they are better informed than most other market participants. So the idea that transactors should not care to bring as much information as possible to bear on their transaction decisions is just silly.

Given these observations, not to mention common sense, it is clear that institutional transactors—even those who trade in liquid markets—should employ valuation mechanisms beyond simply observing and accepting the current market price. Models and information generated by models are critical tools for supporting market transaction activities, and institutions who can provide more and better quality information to their traders can be presumed to experience performance gains, even if those gains may be very difficult to quantify.

NOTES

1. We discuss an example of this, using auto insurance pricing, in Chapter 9.
2. A notable exception might be called *price observers*, who trade speculatively based on price movements alone. The ability of these traders to discern future price movements from past price movements by assessing the psychology of market participants seems to be mixed and is beyond the scope of this discussion.
3. Riccardo Rebonato, "Theory and Practice of Model Risk Management," Quantitative Research Centre (QUARC) of the Royal Bank of Scotland, Oxford Financial Research Centre, Oxford University (2003): 5.

CHAPTER 6

Data Risk
Measurement

ike models, data is both useful and—to the extent that it does get used—risky. As discussed extensively in Chapter 2, the main causes and mitigation of data risk will be reflected in the firm's overall data and information processing infrastructure. To the extent that that design supports the controlled acquisition of data, a unidirectional flow of data from the core out to the multiple end-users, and the efficiency of targeted data quality control points, the overall data risk will be low. For firms without infrastructures that boast these features, the risks will likely be higher and may be extremely difficult to assess with any rigor. For firms with scattered systems, multiple points of entry, and down-stream data quality mechanisms, proactive data risk management will be difficult, and the measurement of risks may need to be gleaned from the frequency of observed errors and the intensity and scope of ongoing reconciliation processes. For most institutions, organized data quality programs are in their infancy and often seriously constrained by system configuration deficiencies. Again, the observations of regulators are apropos:

> 3.14. Data dictionary: Firms had started to create data dictionaries, which was seen as a good approach to understanding and classifying data. However, few firms

could evidence the effectiveness of existing procedures to ensure the timely maintenance and consistent use of the data dictionary across the firm.

3.15. Data quality: Few firms provided sufficient evidence to show that data used in their internal model was accurate, complete and appropriate.[1]

As mentioned in Chapter 5, the tools of information theory can prove useful in assessing various types of risk, including data risk. From an end-use perspective, as with models and model risk, a firm could establish performance-based measures for data-dependent processes that include failure thresholds. Through this exercise, the concept of data risk is made concrete—data risk is the likelihood that data deficiencies will cause the failure of a data-dependent process. Failure may result either from poor data quality or from the interruption of a key data flow. While data interruption is an operational risk somewhat beyond the scope of this book, data quality management is a core information processing component with direct links to performance, competitive position, and reputational capital.

Lastly, while incorrect or poor data may cause problems, and while data interruption is an important and well-recognized component of business continuity risk, increasingly the biggest data-related risk for large financial institutions is data theft and subsequent illicit use or redistribution. The cost in terms of reputational damage from a major customer data leak could be severe, particularly as customer notification laws have been recently enacted in many countries (including Japan and South Korea), in the eurozone, and in most states in the United States. And while the legal landscape in terms of direct fines and penalties associated with such breaches is evolving, the risk of such fines and the threat of civil suits that could involve hundreds of thousands, if not millions, of litigants are both quite real. One retailer with a slightly ironic name recently suffered a major breach and loss of consumer data and is estimating its liability expense at around $150 million.[2] Cyber security, as a topic, is beyond the scope of this book and beyond the ability of the author to offer any valuable insights or suggestions. However, it should be observed that expertise in data management and the centralized data model, for all of their competitive benefits, could increase vulnerability and make an institution a better target for cybercriminals. Obviously, vast amounts of high quality data that is all stored in one integrated structure is as appealing to thieves as it is to the firm and its commercial constituents, as recent high-profile incidents attest. Therefore, care ought to be taken to not create too attractive a target without the appropriate level of investment in security.

STRATEGIC DATA ACQUISITION

A big part of data risk management is making sure that data enters the system deliberately and under controlled conditions. Under the assumption that each institution will require vastly higher amounts of data, and that the data will need to be highly structured to maximize the information that can be created from it, the data acquisition strategy has to include its own infrastructure and data processing capabilities. The acquisition of data of an increasingly wide array of types and from a rapidly evolving set of source types will present ongoing engineering challenges. Given that the goal is to control and manage the firm's stock of data holistically, the biggest challenge (aside from identifying what data to acquire) will be to fit new data types into the highly normalized central data architecture, process the data from its raw form into the required form, and to inventory and check the quality of the data at some point prior to redistribution within the system.

As discussed in Chapter 2, a key input into designing the institution's core system is deciding about current and future scale in terms of total data volume. But an informed view of how much data the system should be designed to handle needs to include some estimation of what the sources of that data will be. Each of these various sources of information will present its own set of challenges in integrating it into the core system, and some of the largest volume growth may be from sources that have historically formed only a small fraction of the data flowing into the system. These may include private databases that are in the process of being created, including commercial obligor financial and performance data, social media sources, telematic and other commercial physical sensing and data generation devices, and more varied personal and behavioral data captured from smartphones and other portable devices. As shown in Figure 6.1, these various types of data sources may need specialized preprocessing to allow them to be

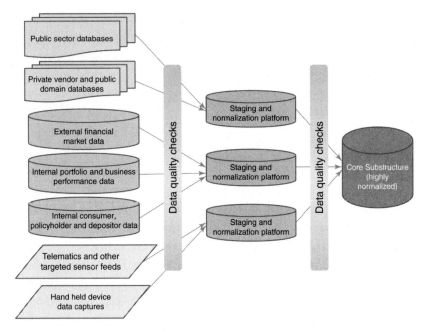

Figure 6.1 Data Acquisition System Schema

incorporated into the core data architecture and hence may require physical staging areas within which those processes can be developed and deployed. Of course, Figure 6.1 is just illustrative—the number of useful sources of data on the left-hand side may number in the hundreds or even thousands. Moreover, similarly to the analytic layer on the other side of the data model, data sources and their technologies are likely to be evolving at a very rapid rate—certainly far more rapidly than the underlying data storage model and technology are changing. To manage such data growth while simultaneously managing data risk will require sufficient resourcing of the data acquisition function, the involvement of the senior system design engineers, and the effective application of source-level data quality controls. We discuss strategic data acquisition in more detail in Chapter 8.

THE INFORMATION CONVERSION RATE

As described in Chapter 2, the conversion of data into information involves the ability to characterize selected facts and forecasts probabilistically. We have discussed the critical role that models play in effecting that conversion. It is self-evident that access to better and more timely information enables better business decision making. And while higher volumes and quality of information in no way guarantee better decision making, the efficiency of information creation can be viewed as an end in itself and one that could support some quantitative measurement under the right circumstances. The circumstances that support this include, of course, a controlled information processing infrastructure.

As we have already pointed out, a benefit of the single-source data model described in Chapter 2 is that the accumulation of data into the firm can be controlled and measured. Diagnostics to calculate data accumulation within an identified industrial database are commercially available (often through the vendors themselves) and relatively easy to use, so obtaining real-time data stock measures is cheap for a firm that uses one central repository. On the other hand, such measures will not be fully reliable, nor are they easy to apply if the data is not highly normalized and centralized and the measures applied to that single point of origination. If data volume measures are applied to multiple decentralized models and data marts and then summed, those measures will be inflated by duplication and the accumulation of redundant identifiers. The augmented data model contains a dedicated storage architecture for model outputs, which are accumulated and also time-stamped to reflect when they were created. Using the time stamps, it is easy to calculate a volume measure of the flow of outputs per unit of time.

To create reasonable approximation metrics for the information conversion rate, it would suffice to ensure that the underlying data model has just two basic features: a comprehensive inventory of stored raw data, and a process by which all model outputs are stored and associated with basic metadata, such as when the model output was produced, what the inputs were, and what the uses were. Armed with these, we could calculate a gross rate as *model outputs produced in a given period/total stock of data* or a net rate as *model outputs produced in a given period/associated model inputs* or rates that lever the information quantity or quality in the models themselves, emanating from the model validation process. Alternatively, we could exclude from the denominator historical data beyond some archive date if the historical data is believed to have limited relevance, just to keep the measure more timely and dynamic. Such metrics can help measure the growth of analytic output and the efficacy of data acquisition strategies over time. They could even be created by segments of the business to assess resource allocations and to evaluate LOB strategies. Importantly, with the data architecture in place, metrics of this type can be written as elementary queries so that the cost of producing them on an ongoing basis is close to zero.

OTHER APPROACHES FOR DATA RISK ASSESSMENT

As discussed further in this chapter, it can be extremely helpful to map out the broader information flows that the institution needs to support its operations by category, including such things as required disclosures, marketing communications, pricing-related communications, and so on. With key information flows so mapped, specific data elements could also be associated with each. Through lens of the many-to-many mapping, we could see the extent to which the data risks *across* processes are concentrated (or not) in a subset of high-leverage data. Then those very critical elements can be targeted for higher levels of control. In a centralized model, the combined-use view can help bring improvements to data that might not otherwise warrant it on a stand-alone basis. For example, modelers can often comfortably control or ignore a certain amount of error in their modeling data. So if, for example, pricing teams were modeling risk characteristics by geography, a certain amount of error in the zip code field might not be worth remediating. But if those same zip code errors were causing problems in AML processing and slowdowns in accounts receivable, they might be worth remediating, creating slightly improved geographic risk modeling as a by-product.

As discussed in Chapter 4, information theory provides a variety of concepts that can be leveraged to establish control mechanisms for those parts of an institution's activities that can be cast as quantitative communication processes. Models, as we have seen, can be cast in this way under certain conditions. Data itself can be more easily viewed through this lens, and in fact, some of the tools that were developed to support modern digital communication technologies have direct application in the data quality area. We have seen that to leverage the information entropy concept we had to make the assumption that the signal in which we are interested is coming from an *ergodic* source. We have acknowledged that this assumption was at best heroic in the predictive modeling case, but perhaps far less heroic in the data quality context, with the level of heroism varying from field to field. To take our previous example of zip codes, it is true that new zip codes are added from time to time. But that growth is limited and is itself governed by fairly well-structured rules. So the flow of zip code data through a process is a very close replication of a noisy signal from an ergodic source. The set of zip codes expected is (nearly) fixed and can be expected to flow with a very stable set of probabilities. That is, we can evaluate the likelihood of seeing the sequence of five digits that represents each zip code and use that to create an entropy measure for the zip code flow. What does this accomplish? We have already seen that the cheapest way to eliminate data errors is to have access to an authoritative reference set. But when the set is flowing at high volume and changing at high frequency, an authoritative reference set is less likely to exist and harder to apply. We can easily filter out false zip codes using an authoritative reference set, but how do we gauge the accuracy of the association between valid zip codes and associated counterparties? Sample testing is part of the answer since it can establish a baseline, but it is costly. Once a baseline has been established, however, entropy measures can provide low-cost insight into whether there is deterioration, improvement, or no change in the quality of an appropriately characterized data element.

NOTES

1. Financial Services Authority, *Solvency II: Internal Model Approval Process Thematic Review Findings* (February 2011): 8, www.macs.hw.ac.uk/~andrewc/erm2/reading/FSA .InternalModelApprovalProcess.pdf.
2. "Retailer Target Expects Data Breach to Cost $148 Million," *SC Magazine*, August 5, 2014.

CHAPTER 7

A Higher Level of Integration

M ost of the foregoing discussion focused on the physical aspects of data and information processing and on the human capital requirements of managing those physical processes. However, while these core competencies are fundamental to supporting a more competitive product and service stack, the physical processing infrastructure can be viewed as nested in multiple superstructures. These include a finance and accounting view of the firm, a risk view of the firm, various process views, and a meta-information view (a view of the firm's infrastructure), all of which are required to manage the firm's operations. Processes for which it may be helpful to actively manage the information-creating infrastructure include financial disclosures, capital planning and stress testing, internal performance measurement, customer marketing programs, and others. These critical processes span multiple information flows, infrastructure components, and organization subgroups, and holistic management of them requires the ability to see and assess all of the critical core and supporting sub-processes, inputs, and infrastructure. To obtain these more integrated views of the institution's operations requires a significant amount of cross-functional knowledge pooling as well as some specialized tools and techniques.

ALTERNATE VIEWS OF INTEGRATION

Most of the discussion presented so far has focused on the physical management of data, and the processing flow of data as it makes its way into the information-creating activity of the analytic layer. Certainly, the physical capabilities for storing and processing information are foundational. But the view of information creation and information management could be organized along lines other than the physical flow of data. These other organizing principles can help the institution to identify constraints, manage its ongoing resource investments, and extract and create value. They include, among others:

- Systems
- Processes
- Models
- Organizational units
- Product lines
- Compliance

When we say an *integrated view*, we mean the ability to identify and evaluate information processing capabilities along these various dimensions, singly or in combination. The first step in developing a more integrated view of the firm's general information processing is the capacity to develop and maintain inventories of the components contained in the multiple dimensions of firm operation bulleted above. With these in hand, an integrated view is enabled and can throw off a variety of high-value strategic information.

IDENTIFYING KEY INFORMATION CYCLES

From a management perspective, it may be useful to break out the information processing activities into some specific information flows defined by essential corporate function. This helps to organize the component parts, data, systems, models, platforms, function groups, and the like by their association with these flows. For most of these, identified at a high level, we could use the term *information cycles* because each is ongoing and involves both large amounts of data being converted into information and large flows of information into and out of the firm. This association is informative in both directions. First, managing these key information cycles represents a significant proportion of the overall management of the institution, and while each of these cycles has its own strategic and tactical objectives, associating them with their internal underlying processes and associated infrastructure can help the firm to make more cohesive tactical decisions, especially with respect to resource allocation and aggregate infrastructure investment. Second, knowing what component parts support each flow allows for a more comprehensive analysis of process efficiency and risk. After creating this segmentation of information flows, we can take the next steps: creating a taxonomy of risks to the firm (based on what would happen if any of the key information flows were interrupted or impaired), and then associating source data, platforms and applications, and models with the information flows that they support.

For banks and insurance companies, a central component of their economic activities includes raising capital from depositors and policyholders and lending out those funds, or in the case of insurance companies, investing those funds in such a way that potential future claims can be comfortably covered by asset sales if necessary. This set of activities is supported by product and service design, marketing, and pricing, all of which are supported by an array of information processing activities. In particular, the quality and efficiency of customer interactions are now overwhelmingly functions of a firm's capability in web-service provision and handheld device applications. These technologies are crucial not only for maintaining a competitive customer experience but also for strategic data acquisition. Therefore these information cycles need dedicated strategies that integrate the technological challenges of the interface technologies with the core storage and retrieval system design features.

Separately, most institutions rely on ready access to capital markets to manage wholesale funding and cash management needs and to provide financial flexibility to support business development and other strategic needs. This requires a separate set of information flows directed toward informing market participants about the health and financial strength of the institution, participants that include the investors themselves, rating agencies, and industry analysts. The primary vehicles for this communication are the pricing of products and services, press releases, and publicly observable actions and activities. As a group, these information flows emanate from within the firm, with the cyclical return flow being composed primarily of the observable behavior of depositors, policyholders, and investors, but also including active market intelligence-gathering that may bear on the potential future behavior of depositors, policyholders, and investors. Most of this outflow of information is deliberate and controlled. Most of the inflow of information is also controlled in the sense that the institution chooses what information it will collect and how it will be organized and stored. From an information management perspective, it may make sense for the institution to manage these inflows and outflows somewhat independently, meaning that each has its own inventories of data, systems, models, platforms, and so on. Practically speaking, this is most easily handled by having a comprehensive multidimensional inventory at the firm level and tagging it, component by component, to establish the associations with these high-level information flows.

To make this a bit more concrete, consider the CCAR process, a component of the lower left-hand box in Figure 7.1. Mandatory CCAR reports are the end results of complex processes that involve the movement of significant amounts of data, the application of an array of models, and the insertion (at multiple points) of expert judgment and subjective analyses. An integrated process map for CCAR should include the complete flow of information, including the physical data flow, the decision points and data processing steps, the models used and supporting information for them, and the platforms and other infrastructure that support each step of the process. For this, as for other processes, each model in the inventory used to produce CCAR results should be flagged as such. Since an effective model inventory should include detailed linked or digitized model input data lists, one could simply use the flagged model list to back into a partial inventory of CCAR data. Additional metadata stored in the integration system should allow this CCAR-focused multidimensional process map to quickly be recast for an individual line of business, legal entity, or geographical location.

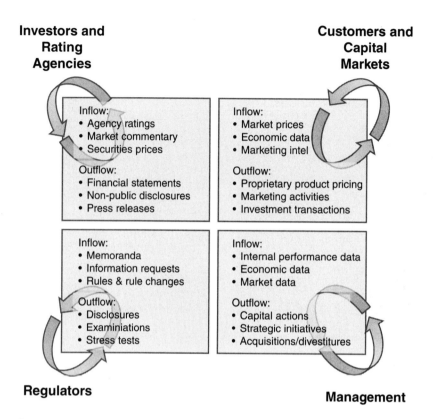

Investors and Rating Agencies

Inflow:
• Agency ratings
• Market commentary
• Securities prices

Outflow:
• Financial statements
• Non-public disclosures
• Press releases

Customers and Capital Markets

Inflow:
• Market prices
• Economic data
• Marketing intel

Outflow:
• Proprietary product pricing
• Marketing activities
• Investment transactions

Inflow:
• Memoranda
• Information requests
• Rules & rule changes

Outflow:
• Disclosures
• Examiniations
• Stress tests

Inflow:
• Internal performance data
• Economic data
• Market data

Outflow:
• Capital actions
• Strategic initiatives
• Acquisitions/divestitures

Regulators

Management

Figure 7.1 Key Information Cycles

AN INTEGRATED PHYSICAL VIEW

A good starting point for building a multidimensional view of the information processing complex is the physical infrastructure—partly because it's so central, and partly because it is likely to have decent supporting documentation already in place. In Chapter 3 we emphasized the role of the physical storage and delivery system as being the provider of data to a loosely defined analytic layer. Integration aside, the complete physical view is an important management tool for an information processing firm. Effective deployment of infrastructure does more than just denormalize data to facilitate its supply to the analytic layer. Information assets should fit together to help manage the firm's operations by improving the information flow to decision makers and by providing diagnostics about how the overall firm and its information assets are performing. To make this concrete,

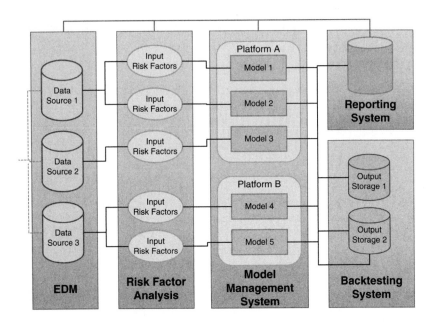

Figure 7.2 Integrated Process Map (Physical Dimension Only)

consider the schema presented in Figure 7.2. This presents a more model-centric view (of a portion) of the firm's physical information processing infrastructure, focused on specific data flows, information processes, and uses.

What is required to produce this type of circuit board view of end-to-end physical processes includes the annotated inventories of data systems, data flows, platforms, models and final reports, as well as the cross-association information that relates each of these component types to each of the others. It may include other intermediate steps that help clarify the overall process. For example, in Figure 7.2 a separate process step labeled *risk factor analysis* is included. This is a stage at which the specific set of data elements feeding a specific set of models is identified, so that it may be separately analyzed, have additional process-specific controls applied, or both. The annotations include the metadata items discussed previously, including ownership, vintage, vendor (if any), control information (including quality and risk assessment), and control responsibilities. Finally, the overall process should be associated with the key information cycles it supports and tied into a key information cycle map, as is broadly presented in Figure 7.1.

MULTIDIMENSIONAL INFORMATION ASSET MANAGEMENT

To this point, we have

- Established a schematic diagram of physical analytic assets, as in Figure 2.1.
- Identified key information cycles and associated each with its component subprocesses and physical infrastructure.
- Created some basic model of the financial institution's production function that not only links income streams to supporting data and models but weights those contributions.

We have the basic information to create a multidimensional view of the information production process. Other dimensions that we may like to include might be information on organizational structure, including legal entity maps, geographic segregation, and functional group information. Multidimensional process mapping has been evolving rapidly outside of the financial services industry and has proved extremely useful for both process improvement and strategic decision making in industries such as manufacturing. The technical challenges in performing such an exercise have gone from impassible (in some cases) to almost trivial as software designed for this purpose has evolved to match the evolving demand. Products like the Mega system allow all of the diverse elements that comprise the full integrated map to be represented as objects, with user-specified structural metadata stored in the system and used to maintain the relationships in the map. This is crucial, since one of the main challenges for making such a management tool useful is maintenance.

A rendering of a simple multidimensional schematic is presented in Figure 7.3. In this diagram, we see that activity is separately organized by goals and objectives; business processes and workflows; the analytic infrastructure including data, models, and data processing components; and the physical infrastructure including specific servers, locations, and supporting hardware. Most importantly, these are all modeled as objects and their interrelationships are mapped across these various dimensions. This functionality allows the firm to, for example, isolate all of the information assets and their interrelationships for a given process or workflow like CCAR. Then, if required, we could quickly filter that view to see the entire CCAR process for a specific

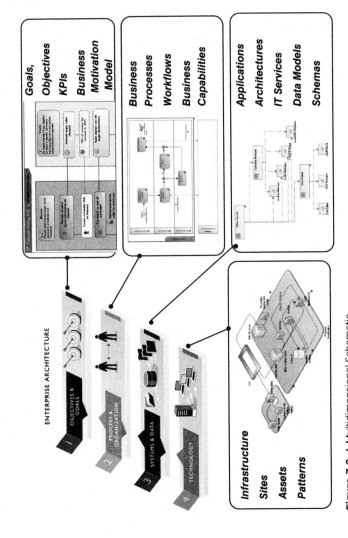

ENTERPRISE ARCHITECTURE

Goals, Objectives KPIs Business Motivation Model

Business Processes Workflows Business Capabilities

Applications Architectures IT Services Data Models Schemas

1 OBJECTIVES & GOALS
2 PROCESS & ORGANIZATION
3 SYSTEMS & DATA
4 TECHNOLOGY

Infrastructure
Sites
Assets
Patterns

Figure 7.3 A Multidimensional Schematic

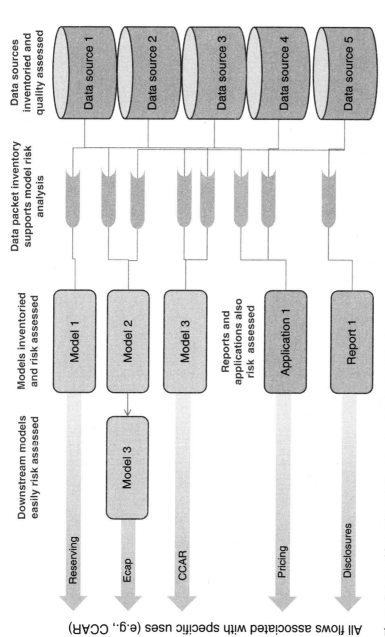

Figure 7.4 An Object Oriented View Showing Data Packet Objects

business unit, or geography, or legal entity, or alternatively, identify all of the models used in CCAR.

An additional object that will be helpful to define, inventory, and include in the multi-dimensional view is the data packet. A data packet consists of:

- A specific set of data fields/elements
- Coming from a specific data source
- Going to a specific model or application
- For a specific purpose
- At a specific frequency

When data repositories are part of an integrated data model (or identified as deliberately external, like data feeds from services) and subjected to structured data quality assessments, then identified data packets can inherit data quality metrics from existing metadata. These metrics, at the packet level, will assist in the wing-to-wing assessment of model validity, as well as the structured measurement of model risk as described in Chapter 4. In many cases, the packets will flow into non-model applications or reporting systems, and similarly, the value contribution and associated risks of each data flow can be assessed and tracked. With packets identified and inventoried as objects with their links to related objects also established, the firm can get a more fulsome view of the flow of data through information generating processes, and can measure and manage the flow of operational risk through these same processes. A simple example of how these objects relate is presented in Figure 7.4.

For a complex institution, the process flows, models, and data usages are obviously ever changing, and the ongoing introduction and retirement of platforms and other system components will keep the underlying infrastructure in a state of flux. The object-oriented approach minimizes the cost of maintaining the dynamic information required to support this approach—however, the cost can still be quite significant. The important point is the following: *If the firm is not willing to invest the time and resources necessary to support a dynamic multidimensional process map for its information processing infrastructure, then it cannot holistically manage that infrastructure and it cannot have the intention to manage that infrastructure toward any specific vision.* For such a firm, we can also infer that their competitive strategy does not include a prioritization of its capability in this crucial core competency.

CHAPTER 8

A Strategy for Optimizing the Information Processing Complex

The goal of this book is not to describe an ideal state for any particular aspect of any business process within an actual financial institution. Rather, its goal is to suggest a prioritization of certain capabilities as critical strategic core competencies, to provide some thoughts about better (if not best) practices, and to suggest a set of perspectives and some mechanisms for self-evaluation. In other words, how does an institution evaluate its information processing capability and take practical steps toward improving it?

In this chapter we consider how a financial institution can develop a strategy for managing the evolution of its production function—emphasizing the desired relationship between data accumulation, data processing capabilities, and physical information assets—that aligns with some predetermined strategic goals related to how the institution seeks to define itself and how it can create a competitive advantage. Of course, the potential exists for designing strategies to pursue both of these goals simultaneously. So-called boutique, or niche, shops often do precisely this: They envision some specific competitively advantaged capabilities and orient the firm's business model toward developing, protecting, and exploiting these specific advantages. This model works. For larger, more complex institutions, adopting a strategy for more than one of these goals simultaneously may not be feasible, particularly when the legacy of strategic decisions and the embedded brand image act to prevent anything but the most gradual adjustment of the underlying business model. Regardless, the three steps for managing an evolving production function that is aligned with organizational strategic goals are:

1. Develop a long-run IT vision and strategy.
2. Target the development of a risk/return analysis capability for models and data.
3. Develop a tactical data acquisition capability based on the metrics developed in Step 2.

Obviously a firm cannot implement a vision without the ability to prioritize and sequence the steps it will take to reach the goal given where it is now, and for that it needs frank informed self-assessment. We discuss some self-assessment considerations in the sections that follow.

EVALUATION

A firm might begin with an assessment of its leadership and vision with respect to self-assessment. Corporate will is a prerequisite for any meaningful change, and a clearly articulated vision is a positive indicator that such a will is in place. While the initial impetus for significant corporate change is likely to come from the board of directors or the CEO, the establishment of the capability for transformational change will hinge on the selection and empowerment of a variety of key stakeholders. These would include the CFO and the CRO, as well as the chief technology officer, chief information officer, and chief compliance officer. Firms with a capable chief data officer may have significant advantage over firms that do not. But the crucial question firms must ask themselves is, "Do these key constituents and their direct reports understand and accept the vision, and are they knowledgeable enough to effect the required institutional change to implement it?"

If the answer is yes, the next step ought to be a review of the existing architecture and overall data infrastructure capabilities, as well as a review of the current long-term vision statement (if one exists) and the inventory of current IT projects underway. This can be challenging, as a large financial institution may at any time have several hundred IT projects going on. The rubber meets the road when the institution gives itself the opportunity to reassess and restate its long-term vision, and asserts the right to reassess all current and planned IT projects against the restated vision. A key question to ask is how centralized the data storage architecture is. Two similar but subtly different problems will commonly exist. The first is the absence of a single central data repository. By this we mean the centralized physical storage infrastructure in a single, highly normalized relational structure. Almost no institution can claim to be in this ideal state, but the range of existing practices is wide and includes designs that by their very nature drive the firm away from the optimum. Data hubs, which give the look and feel of centralization by pulling together data from disparate systems, constitute a poor design, since they do not provide the performance, extensibility, and integrity that a single-source design does. Moreover, by appearing to have solved the broader problem, they can encourage the proliferation of source systems and discourage the full integration of subsidiary and acquisition systems. Many institutions that have committed to data hub designs will have to face the difficult task of honestly assessing whether these designs are providing them with the capabilities they really need to be competitive, and that evaluation goes back to ability and willingness of the leaders to make an honest assessment. For those institutions with multiple systems more loosely tied together, the option to chart a course of phased integration is open. The second type of problem relates to the proliferation of data structures that are not treated as major source systems—the so-called data marts. If an institution can easily and effectively inventory these, mapping them to the original source systems of the data they contain and identifying each case in which a data mart does in fact act as the original entry point for specific data into the firm, then, given that it has a vision, it is in a good position to develop a plan to work toward that vision.

Another good indicator of relative and absolute position is the control of the key components of the analytic layer: modeling and reporting. When good model governance processes are in place, they can be levered to help drive the firm toward better overall efficiency and control. For example, accurate model inventories with internal quality controls can be used to help build out data inventories of higher quality and value. Likewise, metadata related to models (if accurate), such as vintage and uses, can help build out richer metadata for platforms and upstream data processing components. If an institution cannot give itself a strong self-assessment for model governance, it may need to reconsider the strength and clarity of its vision. Similarly to reporting, the existence of fragmented and spreadsheet-based reporting processes should be a red flag that the firm's current state needs improvement. If reporting processes have not or cannot be effectively mapped into one integrated diagram, there is again clearly opportunity for systemic improvement.

The assessment of a firm's data assets is obviously more or less difficult depending on the state of the data storage infrastructure and the personnel available to manage the assessment. Such an evaluation should include an inventory of all the data in the firm's possession along with all of the data provision contracts wherein data is obtained from suppliers (for use, and potentially temporary storage) but is not owned by the firm. The ability to measure the total owned data and associate it with basic quality metrics is fundamental. Without this, the firm cannot approximate its information conversion rate.

Ideally (as discussed in Chapter 5), an institution could strive to place its data assessments on a more economic basis, including a value-in-use component. In simple terms it means expanding

$$\text{Data Asset} = \text{Data Volume} \times \text{Data Quality}$$

to

$$\text{Data Asset} = \text{Data Volume} \times \text{Data Quality} \times \text{Value of Data in Use}$$

A firm that takes the competitive value of data seriously must be able to answer whether it can calculate the second equation, or at least the first. Even a negative answer is powerful in that it establishes the current capabilities of the institution. If the quantity of stored data can be effectively measured, the firm is in a strong position. If the firm has many source systems and a proliferation of data marts, then data redundancy issues will prevent the accurate assessment of the volume of discrete data that the firm has at its disposal. Moreover, the problem of complex webs of systems and data marts frustrates any process to evaluate or improve data quality. The single source model allows data profiling activities to be located far upstream, with all downstream users as beneficiaries. A less sequential system makes it difficult to identify the appropriate physical location for data quality checks and data profiling and imparts a lack of clarity as to who is responsible for these functions. This in turn leads to lassitude and the presumption that data profiling must have been done somewhere upstream. Evidence of highly specialized data profiling and cleansing occurring far downstream, particularly in the analytic layer, is therefore a red flag. Such evidence is both an indication of poor systemic data quality controls in place upstream and of an inefficient use of resources, as the value of any data quality enhancement will likely accrue only to local downstream users.

Assessing the state of an institution's model assets is similar to that for data assets; in the case of model assets the goal is to evolve the assessment from

$$\text{Model Assets} = \text{Model Inventory} \times \text{Model Quality}$$

to

$$\text{Model Assets} = \text{Model Inventory} \times \text{Model Quality}$$
$$\times \text{Value of Model in Use}$$

Again, the existence of any effective model governance function ought to allow for a quick assessment of the first equation. The number, quality, and vintage of models in place is a good measure of how productive the nonreporting component of the analytic layer is. For firms that have implemented some version of a model risk measurement framework, that framework can be used to supply the *model inventory* factor in the first equation. To place this analysis on more of an economic basis in the spirit of the second equation, however, requires a risk-adjusted return measurement framework for models along the lines of that suggested in Chapter 5.

A final point: Most institutions have a wide variety of IT and related infrastructure projects going on at any one time. Such projects may include those that take significant steps toward the institution's long-term goals, projects perceived as immediate need that are unrelated to those goals, and projects that (taken together) are inconsistent, redundant, or act to frustrate progress toward long-term goals. How many new data storage structures are currently being designed and deployed? Do these increase or reduce centralized control and use of data? Will any of them spawn local data acquisitions? Are they adding flexibility or rigidity to the analytic layer? Could any of these create the need for additional reconciliations? If the firm's current IT and infrastructure-related projects cannot be fully inventoried and tested for alignment with the longer term vision, then the firm is at risk for deploying resources that will not improve its overall efficiency, or worse, investing in projects that could act as a drag on that efficiency.

A PATH TOWARD IMPROVEMENT

As we have seen, corporate will is a prerequisite for any meaningful change. While the initial impetus for significant corporate change is likely to come from a board of directors or a CEO, the establishment of the capability for transformational change will hinge on the selection and empowerment of a variety of key stakeholders. These would include the CFO and CRO, as well as the chief technology officer, chief information officer, and chief compliance officer. Certainly, any plan to revise the objective function of the firm to focus more on information processing as a core competency will require a subplan to reorient the HR function toward achieving this goal. As described in Chapter 2, an important first step is to ensure that the HR team itself has enough personnel with technical training in the key information processing disciplines to fully absorb the corporate vision and to craft and execute the hiring and reorganization plans necessary to move the firm toward that vision.

For most firms, the two main transformative changes required have to do with the basic design of its information processing infrastructure and how that infrastructure is managed. We have already suggested some of the considerations for improving both. Next we consider some additional tactical considerations for long-term improvement of the firm's information processing.

Model Governance

Model governance is one of the functions that applies to a wide range of goals and objectives within an institution. At one extreme model governance is almost a pure compliance function, in some cases designed to minimally meet some dictated regulatory requirements at minimum cost. At the other extreme it is a key information-generating function that helps senior management manage and appropriately resource the processes within the analytic layer along with the intellectual property produced therein. Even when placed somewhere in between these extremes, model governance has significance for the point at which information is created that is crucial to the understanding and management of the overall information creation process and includes:

- Maintaining and inventorying of models in use.
- Documenting the association of models with uses and processes.
- Assessing model risk and performance.
- Inventorying key data flows, both into the model development processes and into models after deployment.

In many cases, model validation teams can assist or be tasked with the evaluation of systems and platforms that, while not models per se, require qualitative assessment and the maintenance of associative metadata. Moreover, for large institutions, dedicated model management IT systems are now a functional requirement, which means that the model governance team may be required to build and implement a key component of the overall information processing infrastructure.

While any number of operating models exists, and each institution is unique, the extent to which the model governance function is integrated into the team of personnel who develop and communicate the broader vision for a firm may be a good point for self-assessment. A strong partnership between the data quality team, the model governance team, and the IT system engineering team is probably an important characteristic of an effective vision, as well as a strong tactical arrangement for a successful communications strategy.

Data Acquisition

Our observations about the changing nature of global digital data capture, taken together with those about the natural evolution and competitively driven nature of financial services and products, make it clear that the capacity to absorb and process massively higher amounts of digital information will be a requirement for successful financial institutions going forward. The challenge will be twofold: positioning the institution to be able to effectively store and process far higher volumes of data and creating a mechanism through which the firm can assess and decide what data to acquire. The former is a relatively familiar problem. The latter is newer and requires some deliberate focus if the institution is to stay ahead of it. In the period prior to the year 2000, the primary suppliers (in the United States) of large macroeconomic data sets were government agencies such as the Commerce Department, the Bureau of Labor Statistics, and the Census Bureau. By that time the major credit bureaus were amassing and distributing consumer data and had been since the 1970s; they continue to hold a dominant position in that area today. Commercial data also has now been massed into huge data banks by a few private companies, including Dun & Bradstreet, Bureau Van Dijk, and others,[1] while large amounts of corporate data has been amassed by the SEC and similar agencies around the world, as well as the major rating agencies.[2] For all of these entities, data quality traditionally has been assumed to be high enough not to worry about. However, as standards and uses evolved, quality issues began to emerge as nagging nuisance problems that institutions had few means to address. For example, as discussed in Chapter 1, changing AML regulations required institutions to produce more accurate and consistent identifications of their commercial customers and counterparties. This included detailed mappings of corporate families and their parent-subsidiary relationships, which are ever changing and for which the so-called authoritative sources were being revealed to have widespread data quality problems. The solution to this problem typically had to be multipronged, and included acquiring data elements from multiple sources, independently assessing and weighting them by quality and coverage, blending them, and including internal sourcing and cleansing processes as one of the channels. Thus, in this and other critical areas, the outsourcing of usable data has given way to a middle ground in which institutions shop (so to speak) for available sources of raw data but are forced to internalize significant data processing and cleansing efforts to produce the usable quantity and quality of data that they now need.

All of these factors argue for the treatment of data acquisition as a strategic function to be staffed cross-functionally and resourced as a growth enabler. To the extent that an institution has embraced the integrated data model, the decision to acquire additional data and to extend the architecture to include those additional data types becomes susceptible to a reasonable (if approximate) cost-benefit analysis, which requires core system engineers to be part of the strategic data acquisition process. The importance of this should be understood against the backdrop of the key features of the competitive landscape discussed in the introduction. Briefly, they are:

- The amount of data available to be acquired is growing at an enormous rate, far outstripping the growth in data generated internally by even the largest financial institutions.

- More and different types of data can support more and better models, throwing off more information for decision makers.

- Market share and profitability can hinge very directly on a firm's comparative advantage in information creation, so that failing to competitively acquire data can be viewed as a serious business risk,

The fact that financial institutions cannot stay abreast of leading-edge modeling approaches without access to leading-edge data sources should hardly need emphasis. Robert Muir-Wood is an executive at Risk Management Solutions, Inc. (RMS), one of the top specialty firms producing risk models for the insurance industry. In an interview with the *Wall Street Journal*, he discussed how technology supports financial models that more accurately determine risk. He stated, "Technological advances are changing the risk-modeling business, allowing firms to create models with more complexity and sophistication than they previously could, while also taking advantage of much bigger data sets when contemplating risks."[3]

Treating data acquisition as a strategic function and creating a group tasked with managing it is thus a good step for any firm with significant proprietary modeling activities. Because all significant data acquisitions will need to include extensions of the core data repository and concomitant extensions of targeted downstream structures, data acquisition planning needs to be coordinated with the infrastructure managers and planning teams. In fact, because the cost-benefit analysis required to support strategic data acquisition is cross-functional, it may be helpful to establish a cross-functional data acquisition team that can ensure expansions of the core data model to maximize the value of the added cost. The activities of this team would include the execution of approved data acquisition projects, managing the evaluation and planning for proposed data acquisitions, and providing long-range planning for data needs that include volumes of data exponentially higher than current storage and use require. Responsibilities of the team should include a range of communication services so that personnel in the analytic and modeling layer learn in a timely manner what data is available and have tools available to search and scan the contents of the system. Part of the value maximization, and one of the benefits of the integrated model, is that newly acquired data can be made available to potential users across the entire firm, as opposed to being acquired, stored and used locally to support a single set of uses. At many firms, the problem of locally acquired data[4] is manifold. Not only do other potential users not know that the data could be available, they may act independently to acquire the same data (often from the same vendor!) for their own use, creating physical redundancy as well redundant expenditures. Furthermore, since data quality teams need to schedule and prioritize their work, the data acquisition team can help with scheduling and resource planning to ensure that data accumulation does not come at the expense of overall data quality.

Managing Overlapping Vintages

Obviously a financial institution's hardware and software inventory will always consist of components added and developed over a prolonged interval, one that spans several years in most cases. Each component has a life cycle driven by its own technical obsolescence path, by the support and retirement decisions made by vendors as they manage their own vintages, and by the evolution of the institution's overall infrastructure (which may affect the effectiveness or cost of a given component as tangent and dependent components change). While it may be impossible to forecast how the overall infrastructure will evolve or what vendor decisions will force particular components to change, planning for such change and anticipating the obsolescence of key components is crucial.

As explained previously, the core technology for storage and retrieval evolves only very slowly. Logical views can be adjusted at will since they're completely under the firm's control. Reporting applications are evolving at a brisk pace and significant efficiency gains may be obtainable for firms that can switch from older applications into newer ones, and, as we have discussed, analytic tools and the preferences of those who use them churn at a rapid pace, so the ability to support the widest range of tools and to quickly adopt new ones will pay handsome dividends. The part of the infrastructure that requires the most careful vintage management tends to be the internal data generating systems and related processes. By this we mean primarily account management systems. These serve as the entry point for vast amounts of proprietary data. Institutions that have grown through acquisition may have many dozens of such systems in operation, and serious rigidities stem from the fact that the system features are often deeply embedded in the overall operation of the respective business units with personnel often highly trained and highly dependent on the functionality of their applications. Nevertheless, this front line of the internal data processing infrastructure is often where many of the most binding constraints exist. Such constraints need to be identified and remediation plans need to be developed, often years in advance. It is remarkable how, in a world where most computer hardware is fully depreciated in just a few years and software upgrades happen monthly, these large institutional account management systems are allowed to persist virtually unchanged for decades.

By simply inventorying and dating each piece of the firm's hardware and software complex, the firm can identify its most stale components and plan in advance for the obsolescence and replacement of each based on the broader requirements of the firm overall, as opposed to the narrower interests of the specific business units where the dependencies are greatest. The exercise of creating multidimensional information processing maps was described in Chapter 6. To facilitate that exercise it was suggested that each component be described as an object belonging to an object class and associated with metadata designed for that class of object. For physical assets such as servers, computing platforms, data storage facilities, and even networks and PCs, such metadata ought to include the vintage and prospective obsolescence date. Even application software should have vintage included in its metadata. In institutions with effective model governance programs, models will already be being treated as objects, and their metadata will certainly include vintage. Obsolescence will also likely be carefully managed by policy.

A final consideration is the alignment of M&A and other business development strategies with the broader strategy of improving the long-run information processing capabilities of the firm. To that end, strategic planning teams need to be imbued with a long-run vision of the firm as information processor and staffed with a combination of finance experts, economic strategy experts, and information processing experts. With such a culture in place, when considering potential acquisitions it will be natural to prioritize questions such as these: "How much data is acquired with this transaction and how complementary is it to data already held?," "How costly will it be to integrate this data into our core data system?," "What proprietary analytics are being acquired and how do these complement my existing analytic suite?," "What, if any, long-term value is embedded in the target's IT infrastructure (or will efficiency considerations ultimately require full integration of the target's information flow into the acquiring firm's core infrastructure)?" At the same time, the significance of these questions does not negate the importance of earnings and cash flow, strategic product mix, geographic footprint, regulatory- or tax-advantaged status, and brand value/goodwill.

NOTES

1. Effective and comprehensive efforts to catalog commercial enterprises have also been undertaken by several central banks, notably the Banque de France.
2. Particularly Moody's, as discussed in Chapter 9.
3. Ben DiPietro, "Risk Modeling Advances for Natural Disasters, Terrorism," *Risk & Compliance Journal* (blog), *Wall Street Journal*, March 4, 2014. http://blogs.wsj.com/riskand compliance/2014/03/04/risk-modeling-advances-for-natural-disasters-terrorism.
4. Locally acquired data is data brought into the system downstream to support a narrow end-user purpose.

CHAPTER **9**

Case Studies

I n this chapter, we look at some examples of specific firms that lost or gained some competitive advantage through choices they made about how to prioritize and manage their information processing capabilities. Recent history provides a long list of model failures within the financial services industry that were high profile, high impact, or both. These include Long-Term Capital Management in 1998 (which failed largely due to faulty assumptions in its convergence trading model), Standard & Poor's (S&P) in 2008 (which discovered an error in a model for rating complex debt products but said that the error did not directly affect any ratings), Moody's in 2008 (which also discovered an error in its model for rating complex debt products and acknowledged that the error did affect certain ratings), Knight Capital Group in 2012 (whose trading software malfunction led to more than $450 million of losses and drove the firm into insolvency), Goldman Sachs in 2013 (whose software glitch caused an erroneous flood of stock options orders, many of which had to be cancelled, creating significant trading losses), Bank of America in 2014, as well as many others. The point of this chapter, however, is not merely to catalog the impacts of information system failures. After all, any firm that uses models in any material way exposes itself to model risk, and we certainly do not want to suggest that model risk is inherently bad. Quite to the contrary, our whole premise is that when a financial institution sets up the capability to better process more information, it can intelligently evaluate and choose to take on more carefully balanced financial and business risks, and in doing so can compete more effectively. So the purpose of this chapter is to consider cases in which firms within the financial services industry appear to have made strategic choices to either improve their information processing capabilities or not, and try to draw conclusions about whether or not these strategic choices had material impact on their competitive positions.

THE PRICING OF AUTOMOBILE INSURANCE

Automobile insurance is a financial service product with a long and interesting history, which in recent decades has developed a competitive dynamic very closely related to our topic. In North America in particular, the top firms have been in business and competing with each other for a long time. As a group, the current top 10 firms by market share have been in business since 1923 on average, and the most recent entrant began providing auto insurance in 1937 (see Table 9.1).

Throughout the first 85 years or so, the industry used published trade data on automobile accidents for accident frequency and internal claims data for accident severity, and they competed with each other on the basis of service and good old-fashioned shoe-leather marketing. During the 1990s both Progressive and GEICO began to ratchet up their investments in direct marketing, which historically had been telephone-based but was now starting to become cost-effective

Table 9.1   Start Year for the Current Top 10 North American Auto Insurers

State Farm	1922
Allstate	1931
GEICO	1936
Progressive	1937
Farmers	1928
Liberty Mutual	1912
USAA	1922
Nationwide	1926
Travelers	1893
American Family	1927

through the Internet. Their strong internet-based direct marketing campaigns paid off and both firms began to gain market share. Up until that time, auto insurance products were largely priced from statistical models whose inputs included age, gender, automobile type, various types of geographic identifiers, and in some cases additional information culled from prospective customers through the sales process. In the late 1990s Progressive recognized that if it could distinguish between high-risk and low-risk drivers better than its peers, it could offer lower prices to lower-risk drivers and build market share, while holding prices steady or raising them for higher-risk drivers would cause these higher-cost policyholders to switch to their competitors, who would be unwittingly hurt by this adverse self-selection. But to build models with better differentiating power, it would need more data. In crafting a data acquisition strategy, Progressive had to restrict its attention to high-volume, timely data that could cover existing and potential customers. One potential source stood out: consumer credit bureaus. But could consumer credit data help differentiate between good drivers and bad drivers? The answer turned out to be yes, and resoundingly so. Differential pricing based on the new richer models that included credit scores as predictors was launched and Progressive's market share began to grow rapidly (for this industry), as shown in Table 9.2. Meanwhile, it also began to benefit from the adverse self-selection phenomenon.

By the early part of the first decade of the twenty-first century, the Progressive advantage had been noted and to some extent replicated by other insurers. GEICO, seeking to pursue a similar strategy, was exploring alternative data acquisition strategies. With few obvious sources of useful electronic data identified, GEICO came up with an alternate data acquisition strategy—acquire more detailed and granular data directly from the policyholders and applicants themselves. The additional cost of collecting this specific customer information had to be weighed against the benefit of more information, a benefit that was limited due to reliability problems and the fact that the large historical data sets needed to tune the models to take advantage of this type of customer information were generally unavailable. But the decision to adopt this strategy was made, leading to a new data acquisition process and the birth of the slogan, "15 minutes could save you 15 percent or more,"[1] translatable as, "Provide us with key modeling data that we

Table 9.2 Personal Auto Liability Premiums Written: Top 10 U.S. Insurers, 1996–2012

	State Farm	Allstate	GEICO	Progressive	Farmer's	Liberty Mutual	USAA	Nationwide	Travelers	American Family
1996	21.1	12.0	2.8	3.1	7.6	5.1	3.0	4.8	2.3	1.7
1997	20.3	11.9	3.0	3.9	7.7	4.9	3.0	4.8	2.3	1.8
1998	19.6	12.1	3.5	4.4	7.6	4.9	2.8	4.9	2.5	1.9
1999	19.2	12.1	4.3	5.1	7.7	5.0	3.0	5.2	2.5	2.0
2000	17.8	11.3	4.9	4.9	7.5	4.8	3.1	5.4	2.4	2.0
2001	18.9	10.9	4.8	5.1	7.3	4.6	3.2	5.4	2.2	2.0
2002	19.5	10.4	4.9	6.1	7.0	4.6	3.3	5.1	2.0	2.1
2003	19.3	10.1	5.3	7.0	6.8	4.6	3.3	4.9	2.0	2.1
2004	18.5	10.4	5.9	7.5	6.7	4.7	3.2	4.9	2.1	2.1
2005	18.1	11.0	6.7	7.8	6.7	4.5	3.2	4.9	2.1	2.2
2006	18.0	11.0	7.2	7.7	6.8	4.4	3.3	4.9	2.1	2.2
2007	17.8	11.0	7.5	7.4	7.0	4.4	3.3	4.9	2.2	2.3
2008	18.3	10.8	8.0	7.4	7.0	4.4	3.5	4.8	2.2	2.2
2009	18.8	10.5	8.6	7.8	6.4	4.4	3.8	4.7	2.2	2.1
2010	18.9	10.3	8.8	8.2	6.0	4.5	3.9	4.3	2.2	2.0
2011	19.0	10.0	9.4	8.5	5.9	4.5	4.1	4.1	2.2	1.9
2012	18.7	9.7	10.0	8.8	5.8	4.6	4.0	4.0	2.0	1.8

Data Source: NAIC.

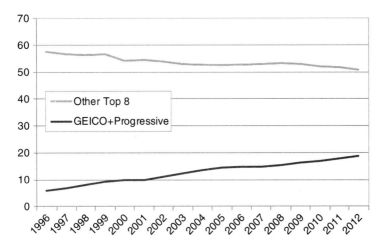

Figure 9.1 Top 10 U.S. Auto Insurers Market Share, GEICO plus Progressive versus Others
Source: NAIC.

cannot obtain electronically and we'll quickly decide if you are below the risk threshold required to obtain premium pricing." Between these two innovations,[2] GEICO and Progressive increased their market share from 5.9 percent to 18.8 percent absolutely and from 9 percent in 1996 to 27 percent in 2012 relative to the other top eight insurers (as shown in Figure 9.1)—remarkable for a pair of firms that had been directly competing with each other since the 1930s.

In these cases, we can see how a strategy to build a competitive advantage based on superior information obtained through strategic data acquisition to enable superior modeling was successful, not in spite of the long-standing competitive equilibrium among market players, but because of it.

This would be interesting as an instructive and well-bounded historical episode if it were in fact well-bounded. But this story continues to unfold in fascinating and somewhat dramatic ways even as of the time of this writing. The new strategy for data acquisition, currently being pursued by multiple auto insurance providers (as well as by motor vehicle operators and lessors), is telematics. The strategic plan is to request insured drivers to install telematic devices in their vehicles so that real-time driver information can be captured and stored. This would allow firms to move away from models that create a proxy

for driver behavior based on increasingly rich sets of driver characteristics, and toward modeling the risk in driver behavior based directly
on empirical driver behavior. With telematically captured data, insurers can not only model the insurance risk based on detailed, individual
vehicle driving data, but even offer performance-based pricing, which
would allow premiums to self-adjust based on miles traveled, speed
thresholds exceeded, or even incidence of extreme braking. This trend
lucidly reflects the basic themes of this book:

- The competitive edge for this financial product is evolving
  rapidly.
- The newest relevant technology will require the capture, storage, and processing of volumes of data thousands or even millions of times greater than the volumes required to support
  existing technology.
- The competitive advantage wrought by this new technology
  favors firms better positioned to manage these increased information processing requirements, which can lower the barrier
  to entry into this market.

MOODY'S KMV

Though not a financial institution per se, as a key outsourcer not only
of data but also a broad array of information and information processing capabilities, Moody's KMV offers an important example of how a
recognition of broader industry trends and a commitment to information processing enhancement as a strategy provided clear competitive
advantages. As a publisher of credit ratings, Moody's enjoyed an effective duopoly with S&P from the early part of the twentieth century up
through the 1980s, with each firm offering very similar products that
covered similar markets with ratings (on a symbol-to-symbol basis)
that agreed about 85 percent of the time, with one-notch differences
making up about 75 percent of the remaining cases. While other rating agencies existed, covering specialized markets or geographies, none
of these had the scale or market impact of the big two. In the bond
rating industry as a whole the distribution and management of corporate and sovereign debt had lagged well behind the equity markets,

whose embracing of the basic portfolio mathematics of Markowitz and the options-pricing theory of Black and Scholes had brought exponential growth in products, investors, trades, and profits during the 1970s and 1980s. Outside observers found it easy to point to the enormous volume of high frequency equity market data available to all market participants to support the developments in analytics and derivative products. In contrast, with no central trading exchanges and with larger denominations and slower trading, bond market participants might have been excused for the absence of a comparable evolution in their industry, which lacked basic input data. But within Moody's a number of forward-looking individuals understood that this situation could change and likely would change, and they began to take strategic steps to help encourage that evolution and benefit from it.[3]

An early insight was the recognition that Moody's own data, compiled manually since the early 1900s, could be extremely valuable in supporting a wide variety of credit market analytic innovations languishing due to lack of data. In 1994 Moody's published "Corporate Bond Defaults and Default Rates 1970–1994."[4] This remarkable document provided bond market participants with the first truly independent and empirically derived examples of what has now become among the most basic input into credit instrument analytics: the probability of default (PD). To be fair, S&P also showed an appreciation for the pent up demand for empirical credit market analytics, releasing "1993 Corporate Default, Rating Transition Study Results" in 1994,[5] but the advantage of deeper historical data put Moody's out in front in the credit analytics race. Moody's pressed its advantage, continuing to clean its historical default and ratings data, expand the scope of coverage, and automate its forward information capture and processing capabilities. In 1997 it released "Corporate Bond Defaults and Default Rates 1920–1996,"[6] which provided statistical analysis and data covering the history of corporate bonds back through the Great Depression. Meanwhile, Moody's had become interested in a start-up that had been trying to bring options-pricing technology into the credit space through the back door, as it were. That back door was the Nobel Prize–winning Merton model and the start-up was Kealhofer, McQuown, and Vasicek, incorporated as KMV. The Merton model implementation developed by KMV sought to bridge the data gap by making the voluminous and available equity price data relevant for credit market analytics. Using the model, PDs can be calculated directly from equity price information under assumptions (and limited information) about firms' liabilities. Unfortunately, the model as implemented had several significant flaws, not the least of which was the assumption that the market value of a firm can be calculated as the current price of a share times the number of shares outstanding. This assumption misses the fact that stock prices are marginal prices and that stocks (like other goods) have upward-sloping supply curves, making the estimation of the market value of a firm far more complex and uncertain than the simple multiplication embedded in the model. For this and other reasons, the KMV model could not produce realistic PDs based on the Merton model alone and needed to be calibrated with empirical default data as a supplemental step. To complete this calibration step KMV looked to Moody's and found it receptive, since it was looking for other high-impact uses for its historical data. Although the commercial opportunities created by combining high-end analytics with a rich source of proprietary data were not lost on either firm, a full partnership was not forged until some eight years later, when in 2002 Moody's acquired KMV Corp.

During the period between the initial default study and the KMV acquisition, Moody's continued to push the firm deeper into the data, analytics, and software spaces, releasing their default and ratings history as a commercial database product with its own software, acquiring a private company's software and data and using that data to produce RiskCalc (the industry-leading PD model for private companies), and continuing to build out a data and analytics business model that was complementary to, but separate from, the traditional credit ratings business. In early 2000 Moody's acquired Crowe Chizek's Software Products Group, which added more software that could be used by banks to analyze the risk in taking on commercial loans. Also during that time, KMV created a minor revolution in the corporate credit industry by providing monthly PDs for some 30,000 publicly traded firms, giving traders and fund managers more information than they had ever had before. Meanwhile, because many of the industry leaders had built their careers during the option boom of the 1970s and 1980s, they embraced the methodology wholeheartedly and created new processes that were heavily dependent on the model. As Moody's continued to push the envelope in information creation it also continued to build out its data acquisition and distribution service portfolio, acquiring Economy.com and Wall Street Analytics in 2005 and 2006, respectively. As a result of the pursuit of this strategy of providing both raw data and data-related services, as well as a wide range of information-creating analytics and models, Moody's Analytics was created as a separate division that "develops a wide range of products and services that support financial analysis and risk management activities of institutional participants."[7] The division has developed into the acknowledged industry leader in this space, as well as a division that produces nearly $1 billion in revenue and accounts for over 30 percent of the revenue of the corporate parent.

THE LONDON WHALE

The so-called London Whale case is helpful in highlighting the value of identifying distinct categories of risk. In this famous case, while a variety of control systems appear to have failed, the failure of an underlying model was a critical cause of the entire sequence of events. Even the broad risk decomposition in Figure 4.2 is helpful in understanding (with the benefit of hindsight) what the *ex ante* risks were in this specific case: loss, restatement of financials, and other reputational impairment—and all were triggered by a single model failure. While direct losses were reported publicly and analyzed in the media, the restatement of financials was a risk event whose true cost remains unknown. In this case, we might speculate that the additional costs borne by JPMorgan Chase (JPM) also established that (under any reasonable threshold) losses under the category of regulatory risk were triggered as well.

The known facts are as follows: In the second quarter of 2012, JPM reported trading losses in excess of $2 billion from a London-based proprietary trading desk trading in corporate credit derivatives. By July, estimates of the total trading losses had ballooned to $5.8 billion. While a variety of internal control mechanisms appeared to have broken down over the sequence of events that produced the losses, an overreliance on a specific credit-risk hedging model lay at the center of the debacle. The desk, located within JPM's Chief Investment Office, had been using the model to short large volumes of the Markit CDX North America Investment Grade Credit Default Swap Index. According to a bank spokesman at the time, staff were "faithfully executing strategies demanded by the bank's risk management model." Initially the recognition of losses led to a restatement of earnings for the first quarter of 2012, which were lowered by $459 million. Good luck and some creative accounting led to this more modest impact on financial statements, but the point is that the massive $5.8 billion loss was in fact realized, and the reputational damage caused by the restatement was *also* realized.

While any speculative trade may go awry and produce losses, in this case three important information management breakdowns can be cited. First, the risk inherent in the model being used was either not fully appreciated or not sufficiently controlled up front. Second, all models should be subjected to ongoing monitoring, and although trading models are especially well suited to high-frequency out-of-sample testing, in this case an effective monitoring process did not seem to be in place. Third, according to reports in the popular media, other trading desks within JPM were purchasing these contracts at the time, effectively taking the other side of the trade. And while this mitigated the financial impact of the desk that was shorting the index (fortunately for JPM), and while a variety of constraints may prevent individual trading desks from knowing exactly what other desks are doing, one doesn't require the hindsight of this particular incident to conclude that someone in a position of authority should be informed when the firm is trading against itself in high volume.

THE MORTGAGE-BACKED SECURITIES DISASTER

Many financial institutions suffered during the 2008 crisis as a result of their exposure to mortgage-backed securities (MBS), and in many of these cases information processing failures were at least partially responsible. From a model risk perspective, what can be observed with hindsight is that the exposure to a set of models and techniques had increased significantly without any appreciable offset in the information content of the associated models, so that overall model risk had grown. For example, securitization of subprime mortgages grew from around $50 billion in 2000 to over $400 billion in 2005 without any material change in the modeling and analysis underlying those securitizations and the rating of the tranches.[8] According to the Congressional Financial Crisis Inquiry Commission (CFCIC) report,

> Since the mid-1990s, Moody's has rated tranches of mortgage-backed securities using three models. The first, developed in 1996, rated residential mortgage–backed securities. In 2003, Moody's created a new model, M. Prime, to rate prime, jumbo, and Alt-A deals. Only in the fall of 2006, when the housing market had already peaked, did it develop its model for rating subprime deals, called M3 Subprime.[9]

As the MBS market boomed, so did the market for derivatives that provided credit protection for holders of mortgage-backed securities—again, with very little evolution in the methodology or information content of the tools used to value these instruments. Both the underlying credit risk models and the derivatives models were used as inputs into other derivatives models used to create collateralized debt obligations (CDOs) that were used to package and sell the lower-rated tranches created through the MBS securitization process, so that material nesting of model risk was occurring both within individual institutions and systemically.

It is not necessary to detail the history of the 2008 crisis here. It is only important to recognize that model failure, the lack of appreciable model risk assessment processes within institutions, and generally poor information flow and poor information management were key contributing causes to the crisis. The conceptual approach, developmental statistical testing, and ongoing performance monitoring of the models used to fuel the boom were opaque and inadequate, even within the institutions that depended on them the most.

The failure of analytics in the market for mortgage backed securities led to the failures of some of the most well-known and long-standing firms in the U.S. financial services sector, including Bear Stearns, Merrill Lynch, and Lehman Brothers; the near failure of AIG; and huge losses at Citigroup and other large commercial banks.

But while most of these firms suffered financial loss as a result of defaults or extreme loss in value for securities they held, as well as the loss of revenue as mortgage-related products and demand for underwriting and servicing dried up, three firms that also suffered significantly had no direct exposure to the value of any of these securities: Moody's, S&P, and Fitch. Each of these firms used a set of analytic tools to evaluate the risk in mortgage pools, and establish *attachment points* that converted the pools into separately rated tranches. The most liquid and salable of these is the AAA tranche, and an underestimation of the risk in the pool translated into larger AAA tranches. Again, according to the CFCIC

> From 2000 to 2007, Moody's rated nearly 45,000 mortgage-related securities as AAA. This compares with six private-sector companies in the United States that carried this coveted rating in early 2006. In 2006 alone, Moody's put its AAA rating on 30 mortgage-related securities every working day. The results were disastrous: 83 percent of the mortgage securities rated triple-A that year ultimately was downgraded.[10]

Clearly, the 83 percent downgrade rate indicates that the pool risks were systematically underestimated. Both data and modeling deficiencies and the inability to identify the deficiencies can be blamed. By one estimate, inflated rating grades during the credit boom contributed to more than $2.1 trillion in losses at the world's financial institutions, after home-loan defaults soared and residential prices plummeted.[11] In April 2013, Moody's (and S&P) settled lawsuits with a broad group of institutional investors that claimed that ratings for certain structured investment vehicle notes (ultimately mortgage-back securities) were so inaccurate as to constitute fraud.

THE VALUE OF ANNUITIES

It might seem obvious that the pricing of insurance products ought to be viewed primarily as an analytic exercise that depends on effective data gathering and data processing, as well as information processing (including sophisticated statistical modeling), for its success.

It may seem obvious that competitive pressures would drive insurance providers to overinvest in data capture and purchase, data processing, and statistical modeling to obtain robust and richly featured models of underlying risks associated with their products. It would seem natural that competitive pricing and product differentiation would have to be based not merely on sophisticated analysis, but on measures of the absolute and relative confidence each firm has in its analysis. In some cases, competitive pressures work to reduce the amount of time and resource devoted to the analysis itself, as well as the independent review and assessment of those analytics prior to use.

One relevant case relating to the accuracy of internally developed analytics pertains to a North American insurer involved in offering variable annuity products. These complex retirement products, which guarantee income to the purchaser, may have a variety of features, most of which represent complex embedded options of one form or another. Modeling variable annuity risk under various feature bundlings is technical and complex and needs to be based on stylized representations of interest rates, equity market dynamics, and complex consumer behavior. In this particular case, the insurer began offering annuity contracts so that contracts with a face value of less than $1 million could be purchased directly through a broker with the purchaser retaining relative anonymity. The price and features of the product were based on a set of proprietary models—as must surely be the case for variable annuities of any kind. Business was brisk and the size of the book grew rapidly. On review of the characteristics of the new volume (primarily for marketing purposes), it was discovered that a large volume of purchases had been made at the same face value of $990,000. Further inspection identified that these contracts were all purchased by the same investor: a hedge fund. This set off a flurry of activity within the firm as it tried to understand what was going on, including a careful review of the modeling suite supporting the product. What the firm discovered was that model deficiencies had led them to significantly underprice the product, a fact that a few clever people at the hedge fund had been able to figure out, people who then began to arbitrage the model (and the insurer). In this case the insurer was able to negotiate a repurchase of the annuity contracts from the hedge fund, but only by paying a substantial fraction of the arbitrage value surplus as incentive compensation. From this case we learn that significant competitive advantage related to information processing may be manifest in transactions between only two firms, *and with respect to only a single piece of information.*

NOTES

1. It is worth noting that Progressive is now purporting to provide the same consumer benefit in seven minutes!
2. The role played by excellent management and superior marketing in the growth in market share was also likely to have been significant.
3. It should be noted that at the same time, NYU Professor Edward I. Altman was thinking along similar lines, and thus was compiling data and using his academic resources to stimulate the evolution of credit market analytics.
4. Jerome S. Fons, Lea V. Carty, and Jeremy Kaufman, "Corporate Bond Defaults and Default Rates 1970–1993," Moody's, January 1994.
5. Leo C. Brand, Thomas Kitto, and Reza Bahar, "1993 Corporate Default, Rating Transition Study Results," *Standard & Poor's Credit Review* (May 2, 1993).
6. Lea V. Carty and Dana Lieberman, "Corporate Bond Defaults and Default Rates 1920–1996," Moody's, January 1997.
7. Moody's 2013 Form 10-K (Annual Report), February 27, 2014. http://files.share holder.com/downloads/MOOD/0x0xS1193125-14-70371/1059556/filing.pdf.
8. FCIC, "Financial Crisis Inquiry Report," January 2011, 70. www.gpo.gov/fdsys/pkg /GPO-FCIC/pdf/GPO-FCIC.pdf.
9. Ibid., 120.
10. Ibid., xxv.
11. Jody Shenn, "Default in 10 Months After AAA Spurred Justice on Credit Ratings," *Bloomberg News*, February 5, 2013.

CHAPTER **10**

Conclusions

W e have sought to explain that the main challenges facing financial institutions today relate to their current and future capabilities with respect to information processing and information
management. We have discussed, using some practical definitions, how
information is created through data processing and analytics and how
it has become more and more heavily driven by statistical models, data
mining, and data analytic tools—and in so doing, have drawn a connection between competitively advantaged business decision making
and excellence in data management and advanced analytics. We saw
how rapidly changing technologies in pricing, asset selection and management, risk management, and regulatory requirements (including
CCAR, AML, CIP, and others) have increased institutions' dependencies on broader and increasingly sophisticated suites of models that
require higher and higher volumes of processed data to operate. We
have described the core capabilities underlying the broader objective:
designing and maintaining a core data infrastructure with a high degree
of integration to support the twin goals of storing vastly higher amounts
of data without loss of performance in data accessibility, and being
able to support the widest possible and most dynamic layer of analytic
tools (modeling, analyzing, and reporting software). We have high-
lighted the importance of data acquisition as a function that needs to
combine the firm's strategic vision with strong tactical capabilities, and
one that needs to have deep tie-ins both to those responsible for the

strategic management of the core data processing architecture and to those responsible for managing the information creating processes of statistical modeling and analytics.

We have also described how financial institutions have historically been weak in information processing, at least relative to other industries, as well as where the industry was in the 1970s—which was on the cutting-edge of these key disciplines. We have identified the source of this weakness as the failure of these institutions to recognize that information processing must be treated as a high-priority core competency for virtually every important aspect of the financial services industry. Reasons for this failure include a persistent cultural rift between personnel in business units and IT staff, as well as a lack of information processing expertise within the strategic decision-making circle of senior managers, and both of the factors combine to foster a situation in which *no clearly articulated vision exists for how the firm will excel in information processing*. We have considered some evidence that weakness in this area relative to firms outside or tangential to the financial services industry poses a threat to the competitive position and even survival of many firms that currently enjoy stable economics and comfortable market share positions. We have also considered how poor information processing capabilities are a liability even for competing against other financial-sector firms, and that the same information processing inadequacies are causing many firms to drain productive resources away from competitive activities just to stay on top of evolving regulatory requirements—requirements that should be relatively easy to meet for a competitively positioned firm.

We have seen how the failure to create a culture centered around information processing has resulted in financial institutions being stuck in a system-architecture trap wherein current capabilities (beyond basic business inefficiencies) pose significant operational risks and regulatory compliance risks—risks that are resistant to both patchwork, piecemeal remediation efforts and a reliance on outsourced strategic and tactical solutions. While areas of information processing excellence often exist in specialty firms, or in specialized business lines within larger firms (such as consumer credit products), these best practices rarely translate into best-practice adoption or vision shaping across large financial institutions. Instead, siloed approaches and the proliferation of performance-reducing data marts continue under the combined constraints of a lack of a clearly communicated vision, the lack of an organizational structure directed toward and capable of implementing that vision, and the persistent IT rift, causing firms to stumble further and further from their own optimum instead of taking incremental steps toward it.

We also have seen how general, and in some cases very specific, failures in information processing have caused certain firms to lose competitive ground or even fail. The proximate causes of these failures include outright model failure, decision making based on limited information or misinformation, and the increased operational risks borne by firms with poor information management capabilities. At the same time, excellence in these areas, and a recognition of the competitive advantages that can accrue with an entrepreneurial approach to information services has allowed certain firms, even in tangential sectors, to thrive, gain market share, and encroach further into the markets served by traditional financial service providers. The continuing economic drag of poor information processing would be challenging to estimate but would certainly include the direct costs of ongoing suboptimal infrastructure remediation projects and the indirect costs of inefficient data quality programs, unnecessary data reconciliation exercises, the failure to feed the most comprehensive data possible into the analytic layer (including the failure to acquire data and the failure to inform analysts of the existence of available data), and finally the failure to provide decision makers with the highest volume and quality of information, and to communicate to them what the qualitative characteristics are. The economic impact of these combined effects must be significant.

Against that backdrop, we have seen that developing and adopting a strategic vision for excellence in information processing is not particularly difficult to do. Viewing information processing as a critical core competency requires an emphasis on an integrated, centralized data infrastructure capable of storing far higher volumes of data than firms have historically held and the support of the widest possible array of analytic and reporting tools. It also necessarily entails aligning human capital with this more unidirectional data model, to ensure that at each point along the infrastructure's schema the appropriate balance is struck between data processing expertise and information creation (analytic) expertise. To accomplish this the strategic vision must be clearly communicated to all stakeholders, including (perhaps most importantly) the HR function, whose internal technical expertise is likely to require a significant boost. Finally, the firm must take steps to establish enhanced capabilities to measure and monitor the quality of the information that it is producing. These include efficient and effective data quality programs that depend critically on rationalization and streamlining of how data flows through the firm, as well as structured and highly quantitative approaches to measure and monitor model risk, both at the model level and at various levels of aggregation.

We have considered why firms fail to prioritize the development and communication of a vision for its overall information processing capabilities, given that it is so important and not exceptionally difficult to do so. While no single reason applies to every institution, and of course acknowledging that the importance of such a vision varies widely across institutions, the inability to perform accurate cost-benefit analysis appears to be a major cause, partly because the benefits of dramatically enhanced capabilities are systematically underappreciated. In part it also seems to be the result of a hypersensitivity to the costs of major infrastructure overhauls. This is hard to understand, especially in this industry where expertise in financial calculus is its proud heritage. While for large institutions a serious plan to modernize its infrastructure might require billions of dollars, these billions are an investment. These self-same institutions squander hundreds of millions of dollars annually on inefficient processes, such as reconciliations and complying with simple regulatory requirements, and these expenditures are not investments but rather pure income drag. Moreover, such institutions now routinely pay or expose themselves to multibillion dollar fines and penalties generated largely (or at least partly) by information processing failures of one kind or another. Of course, what we are arguing is that avoiding fines should not be a dominant component of the cost-benefit analysis, as the value of the competitive position of each firm and potentially its survival should be worth many times the cost of even the most dizzying fine. Ultimately, it seems that the most important root cause of this failure is cultural: Financial institutions do not want to see themselves as information processors.

Even for firms committed to such a strategic realignment, implementing such a vision is not so easy. Overcoming cultural challenges, staffing to support that vision, and managing enormous and complex data infrastructures to orient them and move them toward the strategic objectives expressed in the vision takes strong will and persistence. The willingness to sacrifice short-term economics in support of longer term objectives, and an ability to manage through the disruption that large-scale cultural change engenders will be essential. However, big-bang solutions may neither be necessary, nor even helpful, if the firm is not fully positioned to manage such transformative change. Identifying the direction of the strategic goals will allow for incremental changes consistent with the strategic vision and the reduction or elimination of projects and practices that are clearly inconsistent with the strategic objectives. Without a clearly communicated vision—one that both bridges the IT-BU rift and engages an appropriately experienced HR community—progress to evolve the overall infrastructure and to advance projects that allow for better model development and model risk/model return assessment will be mired in a trench warfare for resources. However, once a certain amount of progress has been made on the cultural front, and in making sure that the firm's human capital is constituted and deployed in a way that can support the overall vision, then larger system design changes that can dramatically improve the firm's capabilities may become feasible.

What will the future hold for financial institutions? It may be that the observations in this book are already out of date, and that most institutions are now in possession of bold, far-reaching visions for excellence in information processing, with aggressive plans for implementing those visions well underway. But it is also possible that at present, institutions are woefully behind and will inevitably continue to fall further behind, suffering from continually eroding financial performance and life-threatening encroachments from outside firms with vastly superior information processing capabilities. Under this nihilistic view, future financial institutions may come to operate as hollow brands, with all critical processes automated and outsourced, supported by model suites for which the analytic development and maintenance have likewise been outsourced, and primarily using external data sourced from massive public and private data accumulators. But more likely, the future will unfold somewhere in between these two extremes, with financial institutions slowly reacting to market pressures and coming to recognize and address their core-competency weaknesses. In this case, the shifting competitive landscape may be largely shaped by those firms that move most quickly and most effectively to improve their information processing capabilities. In fact, this has been the case for decades. However, the importance of this strategic objective in this particular sector has been growing at a rate that may be proportional to the overall rate of data and information accumulation in society as a whole. If so, current financial institutions will have a lot of catching up to do just to survive.

References

Bachman, Alexander, Alexander Becker, Daniel Buerkner, Michael Hilker, Frank Kock, Mark Lehmann, and Phillip Tiburtius. 2011. "Online Peer-to-Peer Lending—A Literature Review." *Journal of Internet Banking and Commerce* 16, no. 2 (August).

Bank for International Settlements, Basel Committee on Banking Supervision. 2014. "Review of the Pillar 3 Disclosure Requirements." June.

Board of Governors of the Federal Reserve System. "Comprehensive Capital Analysis and Review: Objectives and Overview." March 18, 2011.

Board of Governors of the Federal Reserve System, Federal Deposit Insurance Corporation.

Brand, Leo C., Thomas Kitto, and Reza Bahar. 1993. "1993 Corporate Default, Rating Transition Study Results." *Standard & Poor's Credit Review.* May 2.

Codd, E. F. 1970. "A Relational Model of Data for Large Shared Data Banks," *Communications of the ACM* (Association of Computer Machinery) 13, no. 6 (June).

Davenport, Thomas H., and Laurence Prusak. 1999. *Working Knowledge: How Organizations Manage What They Know.* Boston: Harvard Business School Press.

Devins, Michael D., and Michael K. McDonnell. 2010. "The Potential Impact of Principles-Based Reserving on Acquisitions and Divestitures in the Life Insurance Industry." *Debevoise & Plimpton Financial Institutions Report* 4, no. 9 (October).

Financial Services Authority. 2009. "Report to the G-20 Finance Ministers and Central Bank Governors."

Financial Services Authority. 2011. "Solvency II: Internal Model Approval Process Thematic Review Findings."

Financial Services Authority, Prudential Risk Division. 2010. "Results of 2009 Hypothetical Portfolio Exercise for Sovereigns, Banks, and Large Corporations." March 1.

Fons, Jerome S., Lea V Carty, and Dana Lieberman. 1994. "Corporate Bond Defaults and Default Rates 1970–1994." Moody's Investors' Service, Special Report.

Hays, Richard D. 1996. *Internal Service Excellence: A Manager's Guide to Building World-Class Internal Service Unit Performance*. Sarasota, FL: Summit Executive Press.

Herzog, Thomas N., Fritz J. Scheuren, and William E. Winkler. 2007. *Data Quality and Record Linkage Techniques*. New York: Springer.

Janicki, Hubert P. and Edward S. Prescott. 2006. "Changes in the Size Distribution of U.S. Banks: 1960–2005." *Federal Reserve Bank of Richmond Economic Quarterly* 92, no. 4 (Fall).

Kancharla, Satyam. 2013. "Mastering Model Risk: Assessment, Regulation and Best Practices." Numerix Research. October.

Katz, Jeffrey, and James B. Townsend. 2000. "The Role of Information Technology in the 'Fit' Between Culture, Business Strategy and Organizational Structure of Global Firms." *Journal of Global Information Management* 8, no. 2.

Keenan, Sean C., Stefano Santilli, Sukyul Suh, Andrew Barnes, Huaiyu Ma, and Colin McCulloch. 2010. "Diversified Asset Portfolio Modelling: Sources and Mitigants of Model Risk." In *Model Risk: Identification, Measurement and Management*, ed. Harold Scheule and Daniel Rösch. London: Risk Books.

Kirzner, Israel M. 1975. *The Meaning of Market Process: Essays in the Development of Modern Austrian Economics*. London: Routledge.

Krishnamurthy, Sri. 2010. "Quantifying Model Risk: Issues and Approaches to Measure and Assess Model Risk When Building Quant Models." QuantUniversity, LLC.

Kullback, Solomon. 1959. *Information Theory and Statistics*. New York: John Wiley & Sons.

Mankotia, Sanjeev, and Aruna Joshi. 2013. "M(ea+su+ri+n-G)/Model Risk = a Practitioner's Approach: The Authors Propose a Different Style of Model Risk Management That Covers Both Model Estimation and Misuse Risks." *RMA Journal*, July 1.

Morini, Massimo. 2011. *Understanding and Managing Model Risk: A Practical Guide for Quants, Traders and Validators*. Chichester, UK: John Wiley & Sons.

National Credit Union Administration, Office of the Comptroller of the Currency, Office of Thrift Supervision, and the U.S. Department of the Treasury. 2005. "Interagency Interpretive Guidance on Customer Identification Program Requirements under Section 326 of the USA PATRIOT Act."

Office of the Comptroller of the Currency. 2011. "Supervisory Guidance on Model Risk Management." OCC 2011–12.

Pierce, John R. 1970. *An Introduction to Information Theory: Symbols, Signals and Noise*. New York: Dover Publications.

Rebonato, Riccardo. 2003. "Theory and Practice of Model Risk Management." Quantitative Research Centre (QUARC) of the Royal Bank of Scotland, Oxford Financial Research Centre, Oxford University.

Renton, Peter. 2012. "Peer-to-Peer Lending Crosses $1 Billion in Loans Issued," *TechCrunch*. May 29. http://techcrunch.com/2012/05/29/peer-to-peer-lending-crosses-1-billion-in-loans-issued.

Shannon, Claud E., and Warren Weaver. 1948. *The Mathematical Theory of Communication*. Urbana: University of Illinois Press.

Sobehart, Jorge R., Sean C. Keenan, and Roger Stein. 2003. "Complexities and Validation of Default Risk Models." In *Frontiers in Credit Risk*, ed. Gordian Gaeta, 179–211. Hoboken, NJ: John Wiley & Sons.

Versace, Michael. 2012. "EMEA Banking—Model Governance Framework." IDC Financial Insights (white paper).

About the Author

Sean C. Keenan is currently a Senior Managing Director at AIG, responsible for Model Risk Management. He spent much of his career doing applied statistical and econometric modeling primarily in the credit and economic capital areas and published a variety of articles and book chapters on those topics. He has held quantitative analytics positions at an insurance company, a large finance company, a large bank, a rating agency and a financial services software company, and spent time as the IT Director for a media financing company. He holds a PhD in economics and a BA in history/economics, both from New York University.

Index